Flying High
... and Low

A Reporter's Journey

Tom Ballantyne

First published in Australia by Aurora House
www.aurorahouse.com.au

This edition published 2024
Copyright © Tom Ballantyne 2024

Typesetting and e-book design: Amit Dey (amitdey2528@gmail.com)
Cover design: Donika Mishineva (www.artofdonika.com)

The right of Tom Ballantyne to be identified as Author of the Work has been asserted in accordance with the Copyright, Designs and Patents Act 1988.

 A catalogue record for this book is available from the National Library of Australia

ISBN number: 978-1-922913-89-0 (paperback)

All rights reserved. No part of this publication may be reproduced, stored in a retrieval system, or transmitted, in any form or by any means without the prior written permission of the publisher, nor be otherwise circulated in any form of binding or cover other than that in which it is published and without a similar condition being imposed on the subsequent purchaser.

Distributed by: Ingram Content: www.ingramcontent.com
Australia: phone +613 9765 4800 |
email lsiaustralia@ingramcontent.com
Milton Keynes UK: phone +44 (0)845 121 4567 |
email enquiries@ingramcontent.com
La Vergne, TN USA: phone +1 800 509 4156 |
email inquiry@lightningsource.com

Dedication

To Roslyn, my wife of more than 50 years.

She quips that our marriage has only lasted that long because I get out from under her feet and disappear so frequently on overseas assignments. Absence, she says, makes the heart grow fonder.

Contents

Introduction — vii
1. The road to Damascus — 1
2. First steps — 7
3. Over the sea to Skye, or thereabouts — 23
4. Heading Down Under with hope in my heart — 41
5. Love and marriage — 53
6. On the move again, together this time — 63
7. The guerilla war years — 73
8. Wider horizons and more conflict — 93
9. Down Under, part two — 111
10. Victoria beckons — 123
11. Pens down! — 143
12. Back in front of a typewriter — 153
13. Frenzy in the air — 175
14. Sky-high chaos — 189
15. Footloose and fancy-free — 201
16. Extraordinary leaders — 217
17. Pandemic stress — 235

18. Thoughts on the future	243
19. Not quite the finale	249
About the author	257

Introduction

This book is about my career as a journalist, the highs and lows, and the incredible opportunities a career as a reporter offers. I hope it might inspire young people to consider a life in journalism, though journalism today is very different to the journalism of my early years. This career can open the entire world, offer opportunities to travel to amazing places, and to see and experience things few other people do. You get to meet people from different countries, with different cultures and ways of life.

No-one should spend all their time as a general reporter. Being a specialist writer on a specific subject lets you learn and broaden your horizons. Become an expert in that subject. In my case it was to cover the airline and aviation industry, but the media, not only newspapers but magazines, radio, television, and the internet, need specialist writers in a host of fields, from the environment to medicine, from entertainment to crime, from travel to politics. Getting there takes time and effort but in the end, the toil is well worth the reward.

1

The road to Damascus

It's a long way from a childhood living in a post-World War II prefab, or prefabricated house, in the working-class Edinburgh suburb of West Pilton during the late 1940s and early 1950s to wandering the streets of Syria's capital Damascus in the 21st century. At the time, Syria was notoriously tagged by the United States (US) as part of an axis of evil. Why, in October 2007, was I headed there?

Certainly, it was before Syria plunged into a brutal civil war that caused thousands of deaths and unbelievable destruction, but it was already a country subject to heavy sanctions by the major Western Powers. At the time I was Associate Editor and Chief Correspondent of *Orient Aviation* magazine, a monthly publication that focused on covering the airline and wider aviation industry, particularly in the Asia–Pacific and the Gulf. Although it was published in Hong Kong, I was based in Sydney and had been invited by the Arab Air Carriers' Organization (AACO) to attend their annual general meeting and conference, being held that year in Damascus.

The airline body's Secretary General, Abdul Wahab Teffaha, had asked me to make a presentation to delegates, the chief executives of the region's airlines, about the rapid growth of a burgeoning number of low-cost carriers (LCCs), in Asia.

At the time there were no LCCs in the Middle East, or indeed anywhere in Africa. They wanted to know how that market was developing in Asia and whether it could possibly happen in the Middle East.

Problem number one for me was getting into this apparent hotbed of evil. Problem number two was obtaining a visa. The second of these was solved by the country's carrier, Syrian Airlines, the conference hosts, which made the visa arrangements — though only on the proviso that I didn't have any Israeli stamps in my passport. No problem. I didn't.

The first issue was a little more problematic. There certainly weren't any flights from Sydney to Damascus. This was eventually solved by the AACO, which arranged for one of their members, Abu Dhabi-based Etihad Airways, to get me at least part of the way. The route was a flight from Sydney to Abu Dhabi, then on to Beirut in Lebanon. There, at Rafic Hariri International Airport, a car was waiting to take me the rest of the way, the 113-km long Route 30 to Damascus. It was a drive to remember.

Not only was the driver obviously a devout follower of Allah, clearly relying on a higher power to keep us safe as he put his foot hard on the accelerator, screaming round bends and overtaking trucks blindly in the dead of night, there was also the matter of circumnavigating bombed-out bridges, which added an hour to the normal two-and-a-half-hour trip. After negotiating several Lebanese Army roadblocks and explaining where I was going and why I was going to Syria, the biggest surprise of all, perhaps, was what appeared at the border – a huge neon sign advertising Dunkin' Donuts. It looked like I was the only one entering Syria that day, so the three gun-toting Syrian border officials took special interest.

They were not wearing uniforms, just jeans and T-shirts, with guns in shoulder holsters. Although my visa had been arranged, they managed to get across the message that I had to put US$100 into their greasy palms before they would let me through. Not an official fee, I assumed. Finally, as dawn broke, we descended into Damascus.

At the AACO gathering, my message to the Middle East's full-service carriers was simple – get ready for the arrival of LCCs into your markets. These low-cost operators had thrived in Europe with the likes of Ryanair and EasyJet, as well as in North America with WestJet, JetBlue, Pioneer, and others. There were those who declared it would never happen in the Asia–Pacific, dominated as it was by high-end operators like Singapore Airlines, Cathay Pacific, Japan Airlines, and Qantas. The traveling public, they said, was far too accustomed to the offerings of full-service airlines.

Wrong! People have a hunger for travel, and the emerging middle classes wanted to fly, and do it as cheaply as possible. Within a few years, more than 50 LCCs were operating across the region. They blossomed everywhere, from Air Asia in Malaysia, with subsidiaries in India, Japan and elsewhere; Cebu Pacific in the Philippines; Lion Air in Indonesia; Spring Airlines in China; and VietJet in Vietnam.

Something else happened, initially thought improbable. The full-service airlines themselves got in on the act, spawning their own low-cost subsidiaries. Qantas launched Jetstar. Singapore Airlines launched Scoot. Korean Air, Japan Airlines, All Nippon Airlines and others gave birth to low-cost subsidiaries. Ultimately, as was proven in the ensuing years, the Middle East would go through the same traumatic transformation of its airline market.

Within a few years, LCC Air Arabia, flyadeal in Saudi Arabia, Flydubai, and Salam Air in Oman were rapidly growing their fleets and grabbing market share. All in all, the AGM was a success, although some Arab carriers, including the Syrian Airlines hosts, battled for survival.

The local airline had to deal with US and European sanctions, which meant it couldn't buy new Western-built jets. Spare parts for the aircraft it did have were hard to come by, again because of sanctions. Yet it continued to operate and was – and still is – a member of the International Air Transport Association (IATA).

At most of these conferences, the hosts arrange a day trip to a local place of historic interest for attendees, their partners, if present, as well as the media. It's a break from the serious discussions of the conference.

Syrian Airlines arranged a bus trip to Maaloula, a village with about 4,000 people, located close to Mount Qalamun, 56 km northeast of Damascus. Here, residents still speak Aramaic, a Semitic language with a 3,000-year history – the language of Jesus Christ and ancient nomadic people; 268 verses of the original Bible were written in Aramaic. Today it can only be heard in a few places on planet Earth, including some parts of Syria.

Ironically, in this country, which later degenerated into a bitter and bloody civil war, different religions once lived side by side in peace. In one town we passed through, a massive old building stood in the central square, one half a mosque and the other half a Christian church, worshipers happily intermingling.

If I have learned one thing over the years, it is that nations consist of two distinct entities: the power brokers and the ordinary citizens. In countries I have visited like Syria, under the dictatorial rule of President Bashar al-Assad, or Russia, or China, they play their games of international Russian roulette, ruling with a steely hand and their secret police. But the ordinary citizens, like their counterparts in the West, want nothing more than a safe and happy life with a family, a job, a comfortable home, and food on the table.

They don't want conflict or political intrigue. Futile wars such as Putin's heartless invasion of Ukraine kill thousands, not only soldiers but innocent civilians – men, women, and children. Even without war, those ordinary people end up suffering from the imposition of sanctions aimed at crippling the country's economy.

In 2007 there was certainly no sign of the axis of evil on the surface in Syria. Wandering the streets of Damascus in the evening and sitting at a sidewalk café, people-watching, I saw families happily strolling, couples sitting at the tables sipping coffee. Everyone I met was welcoming, smiling, keen to know about my home, Australia. Nobody was talking about politics or sanctions.

I left Damascus the way I came, on a crazy car ride back to Beirut, then on to Abu Dhabi and Sydney. I had been impressed by my visit but, of course, could not have known what lay in store for Syria in a few short years. Damascus was only one stop on a journalistic journey now spanning more than half a century.

As I write I am approaching my 76th birthday. My old dad always told me if you're still moving, you're still alive. Well, I'm still moving and still working. One of the great things about being a journalist is there is no retirement age. If you can still type and someone still wants what you write, you can just keep going. Over the years, this career has taken me to all corners of the Earth, meeting and talking with people from all cultures, colors and creeds.

To me, they are one human family, all equal. I have seen conflict, human tragedy, joy, and sadness, but as far as my journalistic journey is concerned, it all had to start somewhere.

2

First steps

I was a product of the post-World War II baby boom, popping into the world at 5.30 pm on July 8, 1947, not in a hospital maternity ward but at our home at 7 West Pilton Crescent, an Edinburgh suburb, close to the shores of the Firth of Forth. The council pre-fabs were simple houses with two bedrooms, a living room, a kitchen, and a bathroom. My sister, Carol, five years older than me, had one bedroom, I, the other, while our parents slept in the living room on a fold-down sofa bed.

The residents were working-class, like my father, who was an electrical engineer. Mum was a cook in the canteen at a local plant that produced wire, the Wireworks – not highly paid and not lowly paid. We didn't want for anything and didn't yearn for much more.

I was christened Thomas, like my dad, with no middle name, but no-one ever called me that, except my mother when she was mad at me. To everyone else I was just plain Tom, or to my schoolmates Wee Tam, as I was diminutive in stature.

When I was old enough to ask Dad what he did in the war the answer was, essentially, not very much. Apparently, as an electrical engineer, his talents were required on the home front.

I recall a couple of stories he told. The first was that as a member of the Reserves, he crewed an anti-aircraft battery near Dundee, and he harbored some angst against the Royal Air Force (RAF). This was because the only time a German fighter was heading within range of his battery and action was anticipated, a RAF Spitfire pilot came along and shot it down before the gun crew could take a shot at it.

The other tale was about when he was working on a Royal Navy submarine moored in the Firth of Forth. The boat was ordered out to sea urgently, and as it slipped its mooring and headed down the Firth toward the North Sea, Dad thought he was about to spend some time trapped below the ocean waves. Luckily, a tender was able to catch up, take him aboard, and get him back to dry land. Not the most exciting of war stories, but there you are.

During this time he met my mum, Anne, a country lass from the Scottish Highlands. She was a corporal in the Royal Horse Regiment of the army's Auxiliary Territorial Service. More importantly, that ultimately led to me. In Edinburgh, I grew up playing with the neighborhood kids, usually cowboys and Indians or cops and robbers in the woods down by the shores of the Forth.

They were halcyon days, but when I was seven, I had my first brush with real fear. During a school lesson on the history of Edinburgh we were told Arthur's Seat, a distinctive hill that looms over the city center, was an ancient extinct volcano. I don't think I grasped exactly what 'extinct' meant. For weeks afterwards I had nightmares that it might erupt and kill us all. Thankfully, the feeling eventually passed.

Fast forward to October 1962, and I was to experience fear again during the Cuban Missile Crisis. The Soviet Union was setting up missile-launch sites on the communist island, and US President John F Kennedy ordered a naval blockade to halt Russian cargo ships carrying missiles to Cuba.

We knew exactly when the ships were expected to arrive in the vicinity of the American warships. At school, I remember sitting in the classroom, believing that nuclear war could erupt at any moment. I also clearly recall the palpable sense of relief when we learned the Soviet ships had turned round and were heading home, averting a confrontation.

When my sister and I were young, summer holidays were the same each year. We'd catch the Inverness-bound steam train at Edinburgh's Waverley Station and head north. We didn't go all the way to Inverness, just as far as the tiny highland village of Ballinluig in Perthshire, where we would alight and take a taxi to the home of mum's sister, Aunty Liza, her husband Uncle Johnny, and their three sons Ian, Peter, and Allen.

They lived in a remote two-up, two-down cottage in the hills with no electricity, running water, or gas, and an outside toilet. Lighting at night was by Tilley lamp, fueled by paraffin. Water was fetched in a bucket from a nearby burn, or stream. Cooking was on a fireplace-cum-stove. For us kids from the big city, all of this added up to the greatest annual adventure ever.

For two weeks we roamed free in the hills and the surrounding farmlands. The nearby Pitcastle Burn – the farm down the road was called Mains of Pitcastle – had pools in which medium-sized trout congregated. Our favorite pastime was 'guddling', catching trout by hand. They sheltered in spaces under the rocks, and if you slowly slid your hand into these spaces and found a trout, you could grab it and pull it out. My mum always said the holiday hadn't started until I had come back soaking wet after falling into the burn.

Given the primitive cooking arrangements, Aunty Liza was a wizard, grilling the trout we had caught, or preparing rabbit stew, or even salmon, usually brought home by Uncle Johnny, a porter at Ballinluig Station. While it was never mentioned, it was highly suspected that the salmon had been poached from the Tay, one of the world's great salmon fishing rivers that ran through the area and one that avid fly fishermen paid hundreds of dollars to fish.

Another favorite excursion was a day out in Pitlochry, an attractive Victorian town and tourist center nearby. In those days, the main road from Perth to Inverness ran straight through the center of town. Nowadays, a motorway bypasses Pitlochry. Nevertheless, it remains packed with tourists who stop by, especially during the summer months. To get there we had to trek twenty minutes down the hill to the main road and catch a bus for the ten-minute ride into town.

There, we'd visit the famous dam, built across the Tay. It has a unique 'fish ladder' that allows salmon to circumnavigate the dam as they head upstream to spawn. You could watch the salmon swim by from an underwater viewing room. There was shopping in the array of local stores, mostly selling Scottish-made woolen goods, tartan and kilts, or just souvenirs. The day would end with fish and chips, black pudding and chips, or even haggis and chips from the chippy, before reboarding the bus and heading home.

Back in Edinburgh, however, my major passion was for fitbaw – football or soccer – in the street, or in the school team. I supported Heart of Midlothian Football Club, fondly known as the Hearts, the Jam Tarts or the Jambos, who played at their Tynecastle ground, west of the city.

This was a little unusual as my dad was born and bred in Leith, Edinburgh's port, where Heart's bitter rivals, Hibernian Football Club, or the Hi Bees, were located. Why Hearts? I'm not sure but it may have been because the junior primary school team I played in wore the same maroon-colored shirts as the Hearts.

My Scottish roots. With Dad, all dressed up to go to a wedding.

I went to Craigmuir Primary School, and their soccer teams were among the best in the local school leagues. In our first year, in the school reserve team, we reached the grade cup final but lost 4-0 to our main adversaries, Granton Primary School. The following year, in the school's senior competition, the Leith Cup, we played Granton again. This time we won 2-0. Playing inside left, number 10, I scored the first goal and was carried off the field on the shoulders of my teammates. Revenge was, indeed, sweet.

Of course, like all kids, I had my dreams, and an early one was to play for Hearts. But, like with many dreams, fate intervened. By the time I was approaching my teens and after leaving Craigmuir, I went to Ainslie Park High School. We had moved from the prefab in West Pilton to a more substantial three-bedroom semi-detached brick council house in the suburb of Boswall, a slightly more upmarket area, also north of the city center and located near Granton harbor, from where a fleet of fishing trawlers operated.

My time at Ainslie Park was cut short after two years when I was transferred to Leith Academy, the school my dad had attended. I had achieved high marks across most subjects, so Leith Academy was regarded as a 'better type of school'. This move put paid to my soccer future because Leith Academy was a rugby school. We even had a gym master who punished anyone found with a round soccer ball in their possession! It was probably for the best because something happened during that period that was to set the course of the rest of my life.

My sister Carol was deeply involved with the local Baptist Church. In fact, she later married the minister, who took her off to the US where he had secured a position as the pastor of a Baptist Church in Louisville, Kentucky. They later divorced but happily she remarried, ending up in a wonderful relationship with a heart surgeon and living in Manassas, Virginia.

A cub scout in the 1950s.
It taught me the basics of what's right and what's wrong.

Back to life-changing moments. While I had attended the Church of Scotland as a youngster, I was not especially religious and haven't attended church for years, though I still consider myself a Christian. When Carol was taking a group of young churchgoers on a guided tour of one of our local newspapers, the *Scottish Daily Mail*, she invited me to come along, which I did.

It was one of those lightbulb moments. The newsroom was alive with the rapid click-clack of typewriters, the air heavy with smoke from cigarette-puffing reporters, telephones ringing with a sense of urgency, the constant noise of the teletypes spitting out news coming in from across the globe, subeditors scribbling away as they fine-tuned copy and yelling for copy boys to come get the finished product to rush it down to the typesetters. Then the rumble of the massive printing presses as, late in the evening, they began to spew out the next day's newspaper, to be loaded onto waiting trucks for dispersal all over Scotland. It was an unbelievable buzz, an incredible atmosphere packed with excitement and anticipation.

That was it. From then onwards all I ever wanted to do was be a journalist.

How that eventually came to be was the result of good fortune and understanding parents. By this time, it was 1963. I was 16 and had sat my O-Levels at Leith Academy. For years those exams were the bedrock of the Scottish educational system.

The name refers to one of the two levels at which the Scottish Certificate of Education was awarded, the A-Levels being the other. You sat exams in various subjects, from Mathematics to English, Geography and

History to Science. So, as you set out on the next phase of your life, you could say you had seven O-Levels or whatever number of A-Levels. You could leave school after your O-Levels or go on to sit A-Level exams, which normally led to university.

My parents were extremely understanding. They were never pushy or expected that I might try to gain a university degree or follow any particular career. They knew my ambition and had given me a portable typewriter as a Christmas present a year earlier.

One evening while I waited for the results of my O-Level exams, my dad turned to me and said 'Hey, look at this ad'.

It was an employment advertisement from the *Scottish Daily Mail* looking for school leavers to work as copy boys.

They encouraged me to apply, which I did. During the interview I explained my enthusiasm for becoming a reporter and, of course, informed them of all the O-levels I had sat. I got the job. It was great because the Mail premises were a short ten-minute bus ride from where we lived in Boswall.

Not that there weren't worrying moments. After I had started work, I finally received my O-level results. I couldn't believe it. I had passed everything ... except the English exam! Not encouraging for a budding journalist. It was mystifying because throughout my school years, I had always been in the top two or three in the class for English. So I urgently arranged to re-sit the test.

Unbelievably, I failed again. It was hard to fathom but there was only one thing to do. Press on and keep quiet. As it happened, nobody at the *Scottish Daily Mail* or in any other subsequent job ever asked me whether I had passed English or not. It must be said, though I hate to admit it, that journalistic English is a far cry from the world of 'proper' English and Shakespeare. So, there I was, now on the first step of the ladder in the world of journalism.

Craigmuir Primary school senior team, winners of the Leith Cup in 1955 or 1956. Scorer of the first goal in the 2-0 win, I'm in the front row, extreme left.

Back in the 1960s, without internet, mobile phones, personal computers or social media, the Fourth Estate was very different from today. The path to becoming a reporter was also very different. Today, newspapers and other sectors of the media mostly hire university graduates. Bright, ambitious young folks, most of whom want to become instant stars.

In the 1960s, becoming a journalist at a major newspaper was a long slog. You started as a copy boy. Then, if fortune was with you, you were hired as a cub reporter at a country weekly newspaper. After that, you might move on to a daily or evening newspaper in a regional city before finally aiming for a job at a major city newspaper in Edinburgh, Glasgow, Manchester, or even London. For most, London's Fleet Street was the ultimate goal but getting there could take ten years or more.

What was a copy boy? The lowest of the low! A gofer, essentially. You went to the canteen to get coffee or meals for reporters and subeditors. You went to the local bookie to place bets for the racing writers. But your main job was distributing stories, or copy, to where it had to go.

Reporters typed their stories on sheets of paper interspersed with carbon paper, which meant each time they wrote a page, you ended up with five copies. Once the story was complete, the reporter kept one copy, and the other four had to be delivered to the editor, the deputy editor, the news editor, and the chief sub-editor.

On the floor directly above the newsroom, a room with a bank of teleprinters received the latest news from wire services like Reuters and the Associated Press. These stories would come down a tube directly to the newsroom. If it was breaking news and urgent, someone in the teleprinter room would give several loud bangs on the tube, which could be heard throughout the newsroom. As copy boys, we had to rush over, get the story, and take it to the editor.

And so it was that on November 22, 1963, that urgent tapping echoed down the tube. A brief newsflash said simply, 'President John F Kennedy believed shot in Dallas Texas'. It was very late. We copy boys started work at 2 pm and finished around 10 pm. We all know now Kennedy hadn't just been shot, he had been assassinated.

The newsroom went into hyperdrive. The next day's edition had already begun rolling off the presses. It was the first and only time I ever heard that legendary declaration when the editor emerged from his office and yelled, 'Stop the presses'. Very quickly, the headline changed from 'Kennedy shot' to 'Kennedy assassinated'.

Amid the frenzy following the event were also brief moments of humor. At one stage, someone from our parent paper, the *Daily Mail* in London, called the chief sub in Edinburgh to urgently update him on some development. It was, however, something he had known for some time. He called out loudly across the newsroom, 'That was London telling us Mafeking has been relieved!' – an event that happened in May 1900.

The following days were just as hectic as more details emerged about the events in Dallas, including the shooting of alleged assassin Lee Harvey Oswald by Jack Ruby as he was being transferred from police headquarters to the county jail, and of course, Kennedy's funeral on November 25 at Arlington Cemetery in Washington. Sadly, the dramatic events of that November day were to be repeated only five years later with the assassination of Kennedy's brother Bobby during his run for the presidency.

Mum and Dad, who supported me all the way and gave me my first portable typewriter as a Christmas present.

During the three years I was a copy boy at the Mail, there were other more mundane things to be done. We went to night school to take classes in Pitman's shorthand, one of the essential tools of the trade. We were the only boys in a class of girls aiming to become secretaries so, while tedious, it was interesting, to say the least. To be honest, while I did learn shorthand to a decent standard, I never fully mastered it at a fast enough speed to get down everything that was being said, particularly if someone was a fast talker. It explains why, later in my career, the arrival of the small digital tape recorder proved a godsend.

Life as a copy boy was a great grounding in my chosen career. For me it underscored that reporting was what I wanted to do for the rest of my life. Rewarding as it had been to get started, after three years on the bottom rung of the ladder, I knew it was time to move on.

3

Over the sea to Skye, or thereabouts

A famous Scottish tune, composed by Pipe Major John McLellan DCM (Distinguished Conduct Medal), called *The Road to the Isles*, was written as a march for the British Army, and said to have been played by Bill Millin, piper to Simon Fraser, 15th Lord Lovat, during the first day of the Normandy landings on D-Day during World War II. The song goes:

> Sure by Tummel and Loch Rannoch and
>   Lochaber I will go
> By heather tracks wi' heaven in their wiles.
> If it's thinkin' in your inner heart the braggart's
>   in my step
> You've never smelled the tangle o' the Isles.
> Oh the far Cuillins are puttin' love on me
> As step I wi' my cromach to the Isles.
>
> It's by Shiel water the track is to the west
> By Ailort and by Morar to the sea

> The cool cresses I am thinkin' of for pluck
> And bracken for a wink on Mother's knee.
>
> The blue islands are pullin' me away
> Their laughter puts the leap upon the lame.
> The blue islands from the Skerries to the Lews
> Wi' heather honey taste upon each name.

For non-Scots, it may require some translation. Essentially, the lyrics mention the successive locations you pass along the way to the Western isles. Tummel and Loch Rannoch are both lochs, or lakes, in Perthshire. Lochaber is a district in the western Scottish Highlands, Shiel is a reference to Loch Shiel, west of Fort William, and Ailort is near the Sound of Arisaig. The Cuillins are a range of mostly jagged, rocky mountains on the Isle of Skye. A cromach is a shepherd's crook or stick. The Skerries are rocky islets just off Skye and the Lews is a former name for the Isle of Lewis. Tangle, or sea tangle, is seaweed; in other words, it refers to the smell of the sea.

The road to the isles would be a new direction for me. Although I was familiar with Tummel and Loch Rannoch, close to my childhood holiday playground of Pitlochry, most of the other names were alien to me.

But life's journey is full of twists and turns. I had been a copy boy at Edinburgh's *Scottish Daily Mail* for around three years. In 1965 I decided it was time to move on; I was

17, about to turn 18. Once again, my dad came to the rescue, pointing out an ad in the local newspaper for an intelligent and ambitious young person to become a reporter. At least I qualified in two of those requirements. The advertiser was The *Stornoway Gazette and West Coast Advertiser*, a weekly newspaper on Scotland's Outer Hebrides.

Stornoway is the largest town in the Hebrides, a chain of islands off the West Coast of Scotland that includes Lewis and Harris, North and South Uist, Benbecula and Barra. Lewis and Harris are on a single island, with Lewis in the north and Harris to the south. Stornoway is in Lewis. It is a port town with a large fishing fleet, one of the main industries of the islands. The other is the production of Scotland's famed clothing material, Harris tweed. Applications for the reporting job had to be made in writing, which I quickly did, including details of my education.

I had no qualms at all about listing English among my O-Level successes. A little white lie. And, of course, my experience as a copy boy. A few weeks later the phone call came to tell me I had the job. Euphoria!

At last, I was really going to be a reporter, albeit a cub reporter. So it was that in July 1965, a few days into my 18th year, I took the road to the Isles. Well, not actually the road.

There are two ways to get to Lewis: by air, or by train and boat. By air, you fly from Glasgow or Inverness. I took the latter route – the train from Edinburgh to Glasgow, then up the West Coast of Scotland to Kyle of Lochalsh, a village on the mainland opposite the Isle of Skye. In those days, to get to Skye you had to take a ferry, but now a bridge spans the narrow strait between Kyle and Skye. But I was not headed for Skye.

At Kyle I had to board the Caledonian MacBrayne ferry to Stornoway, a crossing that took four to five hours, depending on the weather. The route between the mainland and the island of Lewis is across a stretch of water called The Minch, with a reputation as one of the roughest stretches of sea around Britain. In later years, MacBrayne switched the ferry away from Kyle and rerouted it from Ullapool to Stornoway, a shorter, two-and-a-half-hour trip. I arrived in Stornoway to find an attractive town with a picturesque harbor filled with trawlers and even larger fishing vessels.

It was home not only to the local fleet, but a calling-in stop for fishermen from as far away as Spain and East Germany, plying the rich fishing waters off the Scottish coast.

The Gazette office was in Francis Street, near the town center, and I was lodged in a private home in Keith Street, just a five-minute walk away. There, I shared a room with two Royal Air Force personnel who manned a radar station at Stornoway Airport.

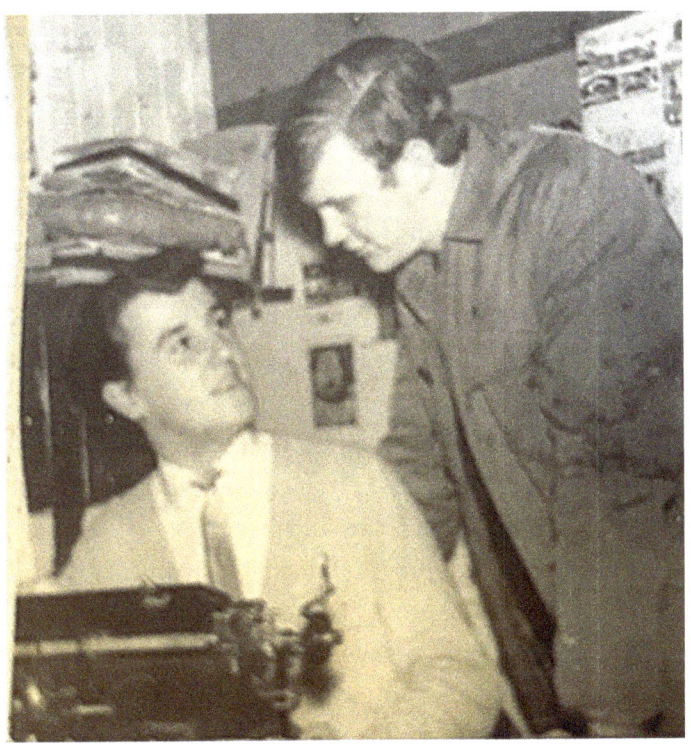

*At the Stornoway Gazette with fellow reporter
Donnie 'Gazette' Macinnes.*

My early days as a cub reporter were a whirl of activity. As the newcomer, I was allocated tedious assignments that hardly stirred the heart – things like reviews of the films being shown at the local cinema, weddings, the size of the local fishing catches, and weather forecasts. There were only three of us in the newsroom: the chief reporter, a woman called Frances, and the other reporter was Donald

Macinnes, known around town as Donnie Gazette, and me. So many people in Lewis and Harris had the same name, such as MacDonald, McInnes or Campbell, that everyone had a nickname. Donnie Post, for example, was the local postman.

Something else I had to get accustomed to: everyone spoke Gaelic, a language as alien to me as Chinese. It was incredibly strange being in your own country and constantly hearing a foreign language. Foreign to me, that is. People would be chatting away in Gaelic and switch to English as I arrived. The language of the Isles isn't only Gaelic. When they do speak in English, it has a wonderful lilt with the vocal sounds constantly rising and falling.

As the months progressed, my assignments at the Gazette gradually improved, although covering long, boring Stornoway town council meetings was not a highlight. One huge bonus came from working there though, one that was to give me far more experience than I might have got at any other publication on the mainland.

The Outer Hebrides were so isolated from the rest of Britain that whenever something happened, the major daily newspapers around Britain, the 'Nationals', called on us to provide them with coverage. We were what are called 'stringers', reporters not employed by a newspaper but who feed them with copy. Among the newspapers that called on us, and of course paid for the service, were the likes of *The Times* in London, the *Daily Telegraph* in

Manchester, the *Daily Mirror*, and the now defunct *News of the World*.

Did anything worthwhile ever occur in the Hebrides that would interest a national audience? Surprisingly, perhaps, quite a lot. Fatal hotel fires. Dramas at sea in the wild storms that often swept through the area, with the Stornoway lifeboat racing to the rescue.

There was also bewilderment for us at the apparent ignorance of Britain's geography of some newshound in faraway London who called to ask if we could cover a fire on an oil rig in the North Sea, completely on the other side of Scotland and closer to Norway than us.

The old Stornoway Gazette building in 2019.

The Nationals were always interested in quirky stories, such as the 73-year-old MacDonald man who appeared in court on a charge of assaulting a 75-year-old Campbell.

It turned out it was the continuation of a centuries-old feud. Back in early 1692, two companies, about 120 men, from the Earl of Argyll's Regiment of Foot, commanded by one Robert Campbell of Glenlyon, arrived in Glencoe, home of the Clan MacDonald of Glencoe. More than 30 MacDonalds were killed by Campbells men, allegedly for failing to pledge allegiance to the new monarchs, William III and Mary II – an event forever to be known as the Massacre of Glencoe. More than three centuries later, the MacDonalds had not forgotten. As for the court case, the magistrate gave the MacDonald man a ticking-off, told him to grow up, and released him without a conviction.

But Stornoway wasn't only about an early grounding in journalism. Now in my late teens, it was also about life experiences. It was where I experienced my first real love and my first heartbreak. Her name was Colleen, and she worked at the local newsagents. While during our relationship we remained chaste, I was smitten – until one evening, as I was waiting to take her to a cinema show, she turned up and told me it was all over. I couldn't understand why but soon found out. She had a 'real' boyfriend who was in the Merchant Navy, away for months at sea. He was about to come home.

I was heartbroken and moped about for weeks, but, like everything else in life, you face reality and come to terms with it. We stayed friends and had another fling later. Presumably, he had gone back to sea.

In Stornoway I also became involved in music. We were called The Texans – for whatever reason, I have no idea – and were the island's first pop group. I was the rhythm guitarist, playing chords I had learned by rote. I never did learn how to play lead guitar, but we had a guy who was brilliant at it. He could listen to a record and, by ear, play exactly what he had heard.

Our first gig was at the local cinema, where we arranged to play a single song on stage before the movie got underway. The song was *Kansas City*, a rhythm and blues number, written by Jerry Leiber and Mike Stoller in 1952. It later became a chart-topping hit when it was recorded by Wilbert Harrison in 1959.

A solo at the movies was only the start, and it soon led to us playing at the Friday night dances held in the Stornoway Town Hall, as well as other halls around the island. We went on tour, playing for dances in Portree in Skye, Kyle of Lochalsh, and Ullapool on the mainland, and we even made the headlines, after being recorded for BBC Radio Scotland.

Under the heading 'Music of the Isles', the BBC's press release promoting the event declared:

> Kenneth D. Smith took his recorder along when he attended a recent rehearsal of the 'Texans' pop group in Stornoway. In the resultant recordings, we hear comments from young people on the music of the Islands, both traditional and pop.

The only remaining evidence of a brief brush with music, a faded sepia photograph of The Texans playing at the Stornoway Town Hall. I'm playing guitar on the left.

A show-business career, however, was not in my stars. Neither was one in the military, although it was in Stornoway that I joined the Highland Division of the Territorial Army on March 17, 1966. Army number

24082515; rank: gunner, not that it was serious military work. It consisted more of weekend camps, sessions on the rifle range with the trusty .303 service rifle, and drills.

My certificate of service says I was discharged on March 31, 1967, just one year and 15 days after enlisting. In the description of 'Soldier on leaving Army service', it says I was 5 ft. 5 ins. in height with a fresh complexion, blue eyes, and fair hair. It also says the reason for discharge is 'his services being no longer required'.

There was to be another milestone for me at the Gazette. In the week ending December 9, 1967, I got my first byline on a published article. The full-page feature, on page 5, was titled 'Now You're Up On Deck, You're A Fisherman', the tale of a day I had spent aboard a local trawler, *The Islesman*, seeing just how tough a fisherman's work was, trawling the rough seas of The Minch, hauling in their catches to make a living.

Unbelievably, I hadn't even got seasick, despite the violent rolling of the trawler as it bobbed up and down like a cork in the swell. Reading that article now, it surprises me how poetic I was at that age.

Let me enlighten you. Under a subheading that quotes from a well-known folk song, 'Oh the work was hard and the hours were long ... As we hunted for the bonnie shoals', the feature begins:

> The Town Hall clock of Stornoway strikes five o'clock on a cold Monday morning in November.

> The sleepy hush of a dawn not yet broken silently envelops the town. Along Cromwell Street only the street lamps, standing like phantom statues in the night, cast their shadows across the concrete highway.
>
> Most of the town is still fast asleep and even the waters of the bay are calm and unruffled. The sad, mournful cry of a thousand seagulls has still not shattered the sharp stillness of morning. Then, as the last chime of the clock bell fades another sound filters along the quay.
>
> Muffled and thick, it is the sound of a voice, strangely disembodied, bouncing back from dead stone, drifting into oblivion over the dark waters of the inner harbour. Now comes another, and another, and yet another. The fishermen are going to work.

Thinking back, not bad for someone who failed English O-levels – twice!

You have no idea how important the first byline is for a budding journalist. It gives you a sense of accomplishment and belief you are really on the right track. It lifts the spirit. I was euphoric and the feeling lasted for days, even weeks. Of course, throughout my career I've had thousands of bylines, but none of them has been as important as that one.

In 2020, during a month-long driving holiday around Britain, mainly Scotland, my wife and I took the MacBrayne ferry from Ullapool to Stornoway. For me, a nostalgia trip. It was like stepping back in time. Nearly everything seemed the same.

The harbor was full of trawlers. The pubs I once drank in were still there. It was wet. Dreary. But one thing had changed. The old Gazette building in Francis Street was still there, though looking a little worse for wear.

It was no longer a newspaper office but three commercial premises. The first was a clothing and footwear store. The second, called Go Fish, sold fishing paraphernalia. The third was the office of HebCelt, an Annual Celtic music festival held in Stornoway which regularly attracts more than 16,000 visitors. The Gazette, it turned out, was now printed in Inverness and flown to the island each week.

Back in early 1968, the nearly three years I had spent in the Outer Hebrides provided the grounding I needed. It wasn't all smooth sailing. There were ups and downs, such as complaints from someone who featured in a story that they had been misquoted, probably a result of my inadequate shorthand. Or the chief reporter chiding me for a misspelling. But these are the missteps you make as you learn. They teach you the things all journalists should be aware of.

Be cautious. Check and double-check your facts. Don't be afraid to go back to someone you have interviewed and say you didn't quite understand something they said or to check a quote with them. There's nothing embarrassing about it. It shows you are being honest and want to report accurately.

But, once again, I was getting itchy feet, ready to take the next step, though it wasn't yet to lands far away.

I applied for a job with the *Aberdeen Press & Journal*, a regional daily newspaper in the biggest city in Scotland's north-east. Again, a major center for fishing, though much larger than Stornoway, and a university town. It was also home to textile mills, shipbuilding, and papermaking, though these industries were gradually disappearing.

In later years, it was to become a hub for the offshore oil industry, a base serving the tens of oil rigs operating out in the North Sea. Situated between two rivers, the Dee, and the Don, Aberdeen is tagged 'The Granite City', its buildings constructed and its streets paved with the gray granite quarried locally. Aberdeen granite was used to build the terraces of the Houses of Parliament and Waterloo Bridge in London.

In Aberdeen it turned out writing for the *Press & Journal* wouldn't be my only job. The newspaper, published six days a week, was part of the Dundee-based DC Thomson media group, which owned many publications across Scotland. In Aberdeen, it also had the *Evening Express*, published each afternoon. I would work one week for the Journal and one week for the Express in rotation. It meant I got to experience two types of journalism.

At the Journal, commonly referred to as the P & J, you started work at 2pm and worked through till round about 10pm, or even later if things were happening. At the Express, you started early in the morning (very early) and worked through till the edition went to press in the late afternoon.

The two newspapers had quite different styles. The evening paper was racier, its stories eye-catching and lively. The morning paper was more conservative, covering serious topics, though not missing the day-to-day happenings such as court cases and road accidents. I was still a general reporter, which meant my fare was varied and sometimes tragic. I covered one crash in which a car with four men on their way to work had driven hard into the rear of a flatbed truck. They were all decapitated. Catching a glimpse of life's dramas is part and parcel of a reporter's lot, but it is not always easy.

On one occasion I was sent to interview the family of a man who had drowned while canoeing on the River Don. His family lived in a tenement building in Aberdeen's working-class inner-city area. My knock on the door was answered by his wife, and as I explained why I was there, it began to dawn on me from her reaction that she didn't know her husband was dead. I had arrived before the police had come to inform her. It was horrifying.

This premature attempt at an interview was easily explained. In the country's big cities, a newspaper's crime rooms tune in to police radio wavelengths, picking up instant information on events as they are happening. Police had identified the man from documents in his wallet and had mentioned the information in a radio message, which we had picked up.

Unfortunately, a photographer and I were at the address five minutes before the police arrived with the grim news. Another lesson learned – don't get ahead of yourself. A quick call to the police press office asking if the family had been informed would have avoided an unfortunate situation.

In some cases, it was surprising how people reacted to a family tragedy. If a young person had been killed in an accident, we would approach their grieving parents and, in essence, suggest it would be nice if their youngster's life could be remembered in the local newspaper, with a photograph, of course. While obviously affected by the loss, in many cases, parents would happily sit down and chat about their son or daughter and what a bright future they had.

Another time, I had to knock on the door of the parents of a teenager who had just been convicted and jailed for murder. They too were happy to talk about the troubled youth and where he had gone wrong. I must admit, however, that this was an aspect of the business I didn't really enjoy.

It wasn't all tragedy; for instance, I covered the visit of then-UK-Labour Prime Minister Harold Wilson to Aberdeen in 1968. Weather was another popular subject for coverage, particularly in winter, when fierce storms and blizzards swept parts of Scotland, blocking roads, isolating village communities, and disrupting communication. More often or not, that coverage ended up on the front page under a banner headline.

In Aberdeen, covering a visit by then British Prime Minister Harold Wilson for the Aberdeen Press & Journal.

My time in the north-east of Scotland was another period of journalistic education, another rung on the career ladder. But by the time 1969 arrived, I was beginning to think about the next stage of my career. And it wasn't going to be in bleak, wintry Scotland. Now, my sights were set on sunnier climes.

4

Heading Down Under with hope in my heart

The National Archives of Australia record that 'BALLANTYNE Thomas born 8 July 1947; traveled per aircraft departing UK on 9 March 1969 under the Assisted Passage Migration Scheme'. It adds that the purpose of the journey to Australia was to settle there, and the intended length of stay in Australia was 'indefinite'.

The process had been straightforward. First a health check, conducted by a doctor in Aberdeen. Pass. Then pay 10 pounds sterling. Migration approved. I could have ended up almost anywhere.

In the months leading up to leaving Scotland, I had not only written to newspapers in Australia, but also Canada, the US, and the Caribbean. Mostly, the results were disappointing with responses that simply thanked me for my inquiry but advised there were no vacancies at this time.

However, from *The West Australian* newspaper in Perth, Western Australia (WA), came a promising invitation to 'come in and see us after you arrive'. Option decided. I flew out of London's Heathrow Airport aboard a Qantas Airways Boeing 707, flight number QF174, headed for Perth with refueling stops on the way at Rome, Karachi, and Singapore.

From the moment I stepped onto Australian soil, I was totally captivated and somewhat perplexed by this country on the other side of the world – Down Under. Straddling the Swan River and with a coastline awash with endless and spectacular beaches caressed by the Indian Ocean, Perth, the capital of WA, is a beautiful though isolated city. By car it is 3934.92 km from Australia's largest city, Sydney, on the country's east coast. Singapore is marginally closer to Perth than Sydney, being a 3,912 km flight away.

I couldn't understand why there were fur coats in shop windows, and people were rugged up in jumpers and coats when the sky was blue, and the sun was shining. But this was autumn Down Under, with winter approaching. Accepting the reality of reverse seasons, with winter in July, was one of the first things I happily became accustomed to because winter in Australia was something of an improvement over summer in Britain.

As an arriving migrant, I was initially placed in Derward Residential accommodation provided by the Australian Government. You had a month to get settled and find private accommodation, which, for me, turned out to be a room in a private home in the inner-city suburb of East Perth.

As much as I quickly fell in love with life in Australia, I was to learn very swiftly that it wasn't going to be a cakewalk. Little did I know then that over the subsequent months I would experience depths of despair and situations I could never have imagined.

The first came almost immediately. Into the offices of *The West Australian* newspaper I went, to see the publication's news editor. What he told me came as a hammer blow. Management, as managements sometimes do in fits of budgeting, had just imposed a hiring freeze on all its newspapers. There was no job for me. Stunned, I had to face the reality that in a city like Perth, dominated by one newspaper group, there were no alternatives.

The only thing I knew was journalism. I had no other trade, and I was running out of cash. In desperation, I signed up to be an encyclopedia salesman. First published in 1949, *Collier's Encyclopedia* came in 24 volumes. They included 10,000 black-and-white illustrations, 96 pages of four-color illustrations, 126 colored maps, and 100 black-and-white line maps, and more than 400,000 index entries. The cover stamping was 22-carat gold, with red panels on black.

Years later, in 1998, Microsoft acquired the right to use *Collier's Encyclopedia* and ultimately incorporated it into its *Encarta* digital multimedia encyclopedia, which it marketed until 2009.

Back in 1969 it was definitely regarded as a high-quality product. The sales strategy was door-to-door. Each evening the team would be taken to a different suburb to begin knocking on doors. The market was everybody and anybody, although the favorite targets were migrant families, particularly Greeks and Italians, who put a great deal of store on the education of their children. We were taught a spiel to convince them that for a deposit and a small weekly installment, no more than the cost of a couple cups of coffee, having *Colliers Encyclopedia* on the shelf would guarantee their offspring a highly successful future.

For each set sold, you received a commission. High-quality product or not, what I can tell you is that I was the world's worst encyclopedia salesman. I can't recall how many I sold but it wasn't very many – not enough to make a living wage. I was nearly broke and couldn't even afford to continue paying the rent.

For a few nights I was homeless, sleeping under a tree in King's Park, with a spectacular panoramic view of the city of Perth and the Swan River. After that I was kindly put up by various members of the Colliers sales team.

As for the selling, I was so bad that I had to be retrained. The person assigned to that task was a beautiful young girl, Roslyn, or Roz. A student at the University of WA, for her this was just a way to earn extra cash. She was selling *Colliers* like hotcakes, making enough money to buy herself a little Mini car and, in topping the sales league, winning a set of *Colliers* for herself. I had to accompany her to learn and witness just how she did it. In retrospect, I can't remember that there was much training at all.

It seemed most of the time was spent dropping into the pub or sitting on one of Perth's wonderful beaches in the evening chatting and eating fish and chips. Another stroke of fate. Kismet. Pure chance. Later, she was to become my wife, and still is, more than 50 years later.

Soon I didn't have to worry about accommodation in Perth. Hans, a German and our boss at *Colliers*, decided a sales team should go on a road trip, hitting regional towns with our encyclopedia. And so it was that four of us headed north. There was me, an innocent Scot; Gerry, whose background was Dutch; Alain, a Frenchman; and an Australian, Terry.

First stop was Geraldton, around 400 km north of Perth. There, one of the main industries was fishing, particularly for crayfish. Much of the fleet was operated by migrant families, good prospects for our goods. We certainly had some success, but it was far from making us rich. Nights were spent in caravan parks, principally because they were cheap.

Next stop on the road was Carnarvon, another 475 km further north, located at the mouth of the Gascoyne River on the Indian Ocean. The Shark Bay World Heritage Site lies to the south of the town, with the popular tourist town of Exmouth to the north. With a population then of some 4,000 people, it seemed another promising target.

Selling encyclopedias, however, turned out to be not on the agenda. Again, we were staying at a local caravan park, and a couple of nights after arriving, the four of us were out driving. I was asleep in the back seat and the guys decided petrol was required. For some reason they thought the best – and cheapest – option was to siphon it from someone else's car, which they did! Unbeknown to them, this was witnessed by a nearby nightwatchman who had taken a note of our car's license plate. Driving down the main street of Carnarvon the following day, a police car pulled us over, and we were all arrested on the spot. Sleeping or not, I was part of the group. The whole sad event was not something I had foreseen along my career path. The shame of it!

After a night in Carnarvon Police Station cells, we fronted the local magistrate and were issued with a fine. Unfortunately, none of us were able to pay up, so for the authorities, there was only one alternative: work it off over seven days in prison. It seems to me they would have been better off and saved some money by just letting us off with a warning. The nearest prison was back in Geraldton, so the police had to load us into a van and drive us 475 km south. Seven days later they had to come and collect us and drive us 475 km back north to where we had been arrested.

My time behind bars in Geraldton Prison was fairly innocuous. Terry and I spent most of our time whitewashing the walls and stones that lined pathways. Gerry, a butcher by trade, worked in the kitchen. Alain didn't stick around. His parents paid the fine, and he was released after a couple of days and returned to Perth.

With no individual cells, all inmates slept in dormitories. I met and spoke with men whose life experience was far different from my own – an elderly Aboriginal who had murdered his wife, burglars, domestic violence offenders, petty criminals. While it was only for a short time, being in prison taught me this was something I never wanted to experience again. Being locked up and having your movements restricted is not a good feeling.

There was a bright side. I didn't actually have a criminal record because we hadn't been sentenced to gaol, merely fined. The other benefit of this was that it brought a screaming halt to my dubious and very unprofitable days as an encyclopedia salesman.

What next? Terry returned to Sydney, while back in Carnarvon, Gerry and I settled into life in a cabin at the local caravan park. Gerry quickly got to work at a local butcher shop. My journalistic career remained in limbo, and with nothing available at the local newspaper, the *Northern Guardian*, I had little choice but to look for an alternative.

The opportunity came from a customer at Gerry's shop, who told him a local transport and tire company, Jolly's, was looking for an apprentice tire-fitter. Beggars can't be choosers. I applied and got the job, even though I had never seen a tire at close quarters in my life. It was hard work, but finally, I was getting a regular weekly wage.

It wasn't all about fitting tires on cars. In a remote town like Carnarvon, much of the job involved handling truck tires. Worse, these truck tires kept getting bigger because of a salt lake a few kilometers north of Carnarvon, which had been mined by Rio Tinto for more than 45 years. The tires from the massive trucks used to transport the salt were replaced or repaired at Jolly's. Initially, I couldn't even lift them, they were so heavy.

I think it was a period during which I really grew up. I had never done any sort of laboring job in my life, but the daily work at Jolly's put muscle on me. The wonderful climate and sunshine also had me tanned. Life was settled and reasonably good, apart from the fact I wasn't in my chosen career.

There were things that cheered me up. I passed my driving test – first time! It must be said that it was far from difficult. The test was conducted by the Carnarvon policeman who had arrested us and whom I had subsequently befriended. With no traffic lights or hills in town, driving was reasonably uncomplicated. It also meant that I was able to attend to Jolly's outside jobs.

Often there would be a call for help from a truck driver with flat tires in the middle of nowhere, sometimes as far as 100 km away. I would drive to their rescue with replacements, or on one occasion, all the way to Exmouth, 365 kms away, to resupply new tires to a service station.

These were also interesting times in northwest Australia, an area that played a vital role in Western defense and space operations. At Exmouth, the Harold E Holt Naval Communication Station is a joint Australian and US facility operated and maintained by the Australian Department of Defence on behalf of the two nations. It provides very low frequency (VLF) radio transmission to the US Navy,

Royal Australian Navy and allied ships and submarines in the western Pacific Ocean and eastern Indian Ocean. The frequency is 19.8 kHz. With a transmission power of 1 megawatt, it was the most powerful transmission station in the Southern Hemisphere. The town of Exmouth was built at the same time as the communications station to provide support to the base and to house dependent families of US navy personnel.

Closer to what was then home, just south of Carnarvon, the Carnarvon Tracking Station supported America's Gemini, Apollo, and Skylab space programs. It operated from 1963 and eventually closed in 1975.

I was there on July 20, 1969, when it played a part in the moon landing, when Neil Armstrong became the first man to set foot on Earth's satellite. We didn't have a television so couldn't watch the historic event but were able to listen to it on the radio. Armstrong was someone I was to meet later in life.

Something else happened during the road trip that was eventually to change my life – a budding relationship with my encyclopedia sales trainer, Roz. In the early days of the sales road trip, in Geraldton, there was one night we were all chatting and, as men do, got round to the subject of women and sex. The Frenchman, Alain, started making suggestive comments about Roz and I got very angry inside.

At the time it wasn't a matter of my being in love with her. As much as I clearly saw her as very beautiful and was attracted, we had only really known each other through

Colliers and the brief period of retraining. We had never dated or anything. Yet here I was, for some reason, fuming over something that seemed disrespectful to her.

The next day I wrote her a letter telling her what had happened and apologizing on Alain's behalf. By the time I was in Carnarvon and my brief dabble with criminality and prison was over, we began to correspond regularly, with her letters addressed to me, care of the Carnarvon Post Office.

This was slightly embarrassing because as I called in to collect my mail, there would be wry grins from the Post Office staff. Each letter had been soaked in perfume, and you could smell them from a mile away. But to me, it was a sign this was developing into much more than a long-distance friendship.

My time in Australia's northwest was soon to end. Gerry was returning to Perth and I decided to go with him. Besides, it would mean I could finally find out just how serious the relationship was with Roz.

It was great. The more we talked and went out together, the more I fell in love. Did she love me? It was hard to tell, and we weren't expressing our feelings openly at that time. I was shy back then, but I became more and more convinced this was no short-term relationship.

Unfortunately, it was soon to revert to a long-distance relationship. I had to find a new job, which I did, still in the tire business, which I was finding hard to shake off. After all, apart from reporting, it was the only thing I now knew how to do. The problem: the job wasn't in Perth.

It was with the Dunlop tire company in the town of Esperance, on the south coast of WA, some 700 km southeast of Perth, a town whose pristine white-sand beaches were a magnet for tourists. As for the town's economy, apart from tourism, huge quantities of nickel and iron ore, as well as grain from Australia's wheat belt, were exported through Esperance's port.

My job at Dunlop wasn't tire-fitting; it was tire-selling. While I had been a total failure selling encyclopedias, tires were a different kettle of fish and something everyone had to have: the townsfolk for their cars; the transport companies for their trucks; farmers for their tractors. But, to be honest, Esperance is a bit of a blur. Despite a modicum of success selling tires, I wasn't happy. I was lonely. I had few real friends and, after paying rent and buying the essentials, such as food, cigarettes and alcohol, there was little cash left over.

Meanwhile, although still at university, Roz and a couple of her friends had gone on a long trip, a sort of working holiday on Australia's east coast. They seemed to be having a whale of a time in Queensland, doing things like working at a resort hotel on Dunk Island, 4 km off the Australian coast, opposite the town of Mission Beach. Or working as deck hands on a prawn trawler operating out of the North Queensland town of Cairns. In the end, her friends returned to Perth, but Roz stayed on, living in a single room at a terrace house in the Sydney suburb of Bondi Beach. There was nothing for it. I had to join her.

5

Love and marriage

I quit my job at Dunlop and tried to work out how I could get to Sydney. I didn't have enough money to fly, or even take the train or bus all the way. Then, a guy I knew in Esperance told me he was heading for Adelaide ... on his motorbike. Like it or not, being a pillion passenger on a motorbike for the more than 2,000-km trek to the South Australian (SA) capital seemed the best – and cheapest – alternative available. It was something of a disaster.

We reached Norseman in WA, where the road between Esperance and Perth meets the beginning of Route A1, the highway that spans Australia from west to east. After Norseman you hit the Nullarbor Plain, an area of flat, treeless, arid country located on the Great Australian Bight coast. It occupies an area of about 200,000 square km and, at its widest point, stretches about 1,100 km from east to west across the border between SA and WA.

In those days, the long stretch of more than 300 km in the middle was unpaved and dotted with dangerous potholes, camouflaged by the fine sand that covered the road and seeped into every crevice of your body and belongings as it was stirred up by passing cars and trucks. We didn't get far. Somehow, on the longest straight stretch of highway in Australia, my white knight managed to lose control. We slid off the road and smashed into what seemed to me to be the only tree on the Nullarbor. Remarkably, neither of us was seriously injured. A few bruises and scratches were the extent of it. But Adelaide was now out of the question.

Back in Norseman I counted my dollars and cents. There was enough for a bus ride to Melbourne, but that was it. In the Victorian capital, there was only one alternative to get to Sydney – start thumbing a lift.

I was picked up by various motorists as far as Bathurst, on the western side of the Blue Mountains in NSW. Bondi Beach was still 207 km away. Then a truckie answered the call, taking me over the mountains to Parramatta. Bondi Beach was now only 30.7 km away. I began trudging along Parramatta Road, the long stretch that leads into Sydney's city center. Finally, a motorist stopped to pick me up. Wonder of wonders, he was going to Bondi Beach!

It was a nervous moment when I finally reached the door of 24 Francis Street, Bondi Beach where, I hoped, Roz was still living in Flat 3. Given the recent weeks of chaos in my journey, we hadn't been in touch for a while. I was worried she might have given me up as a lost cause, upped sticks, and headed back to Perth. Thankfully, that was not to be.

The door opened and there she was, a vision of beauty. More than I ever could have imagined. At that point we hadn't yet voiced our love for each other, but my relief at reaching Sydney and reconnecting with her was obvious.

I had arrived at Bondi in March 1970 with little more than five cents in my pocket. Roz was working for Darrell Lee, the chocolate manufacturers, at an outlet they had in Mark Foy's department store in Sydney. When I awoke on that first morning in Bondi, having slept the sleep of the dead, she had gone to work but left some cash for me on the table. I went out to wander the beach front and purchase food to make dinner for us that evening.

I quickly found a job. Still trapped in the rubber business, it was with Reliance tires at Mascot, near Sydney's Kingsford Smith International Airport, a facility I was to become very familiar with in the years ahead. But this period wasn't about Reliance or tires. It was about finally living as a couple and getting to know each other properly.

We enjoyed the delights of Bondi Beach and had dinner at various rugby league clubs, one of the constants of Sydney life. We went to Sydney Airport and ate there too, watching the flights come and go and talking about when we might be able to board one of these jets and where we might go. In fact, it was at Sydney Airport that Roz finally told me she loved me.

We had a wonderful three months together but, unfortunately, it was to come to an end once again. Roz simply had to return to Perth to resume her academic pursuits at the University of WA. I was left in Sydney, alone again. Once more, I didn't have many friends, only workmates, and did little socializing. In the evening, I stayed in that single room in Bondi listening to the radio – and writing long letters to Roz. Indeed, we wrote to each other almost daily. Long, wandering letters that more and more became filled with phrases like *I Love You. I love you. I love you.* And *I miss you. I miss you. I miss you.* I know that because Roz has kept many of these letters and reading them now takes me back to the deep feelings I had then, and still have.

In one letter I refer to my horror trip from Esperance to Sydney:

> When it turned out that I was going to be so late getting to Sydney – after me promising and saying I was arriving during a certain week – I was in an almost suicidal state about what you were thinking and if you were still there. And you know, if you had gone back to Perth, I would have turned right round, 5 cents and all, and headed back.

But the most important letter of all was one I wrote sometime in late May or early June 1970. It's a three-page letter, once again awash with words of love and devotion.

> But it's been these three months in Sydney that have been the happiest three months of my life. Because that's when the sort of basic, simple love I felt for you became a deep and everlasting love that I won't ever be able to get rid of, even if I wanted to (and I don't). And the first time you

told me that you loved me out at the airport was
the happiest moment of my life.

The most important part of that letter comes on the final page:

So, it's for you and everyone else, your parents, your friends and mine that I'm asking you straight out now, from the very bottom of my heart: Will you please marry me, Roz?

I didn't have to wait long for an answer. It was a definite 'Yes'.

The next few weeks were a whirlwind. I was desperate to get back to Perth but had to give Reliance a month's notice, which I did immediately. Thankfully, given my quiet social life, I had managed to save a decent amount of cash. On July 2, just six days before my 23rd birthday, I wrote to Roz telling her I had been into town and booked my train ticket to Perth. Cost: $62.95. I was leaving Sydney on Saturday August 22 and arriving in Perth on Wednesday August 26, in time for her 21st birthday on September 3.

Known as the Indian Pacific, because it links the Pacific Ocean with the Indian Ocean, it was a three-day, two-night journey, one of the world's great rail experiences. If that seems like a long train trip, it reflects Australia's size.

That reverse trip was a lot more comfortable than the one I had made just a few months earlier. She met me at Perth Station, and this time there was to be no future separation, no long-distance relationship. As far as I was concerned, this was now forever.

At the time Roz was sharing a flat with her sister Elaine in the Perth beachside suburb of Cottesloe, one of a dozen or more glorious beaches along Perth's coastal fringe. This is where I was staying, though it was a fact kept secret from her parents. I had to meet them and, as a Scottish gentleman, officially ask them for their daughter's hand in marriage. This was a bit nerve-wracking because I was pretty sure they wouldn't be keen on their little girl hooking up with an ex-con, a former prison inmate, but all turned out well. They soon accepted that I wasn't all that bad, and we went on to have a great relationship.

In the meantime, I quickly pinned down another job. Yes, you guessed it. Yet another tire firm. Although I didn't know it at the time, this job would eventually bring a wonderful bonus. It was to be my last skirmish with the world of tires.

The company was Beaurepaires. Sir Francis Joseph Edmund Beaurepaire was an Australian distance freestyle swimmer from the 1900s to the 1920s. He won three silver and three bronze medals from the 1908 Summer Olympics in London to the 1924 Summer Olympics in Paris. He was also a decorated politician and businessman, serving for ten years in the Victorian Legislative Council and as Lord Mayor of Melbourne, as well as building a multi-million dollar tire business empire, Beaurepaires and Olympic Tyre & Rubber Co. He might not have struck gold in the

Olympics but certainly did in the tire business, which now had branches all over Australia.

The love of my life. Roz and myself on our wedding day at her parents' home in Perth, Western Australia.

I was back to being a salesman in this, my last stint, and it was probably my most successful. The branch where I worked was in Freemantle, Perth's port. Customers included dozens of transport firms whose trucks carried goods such as grain, minerals, even live sheep, to the port for export overseas, as well as picking up imports for distribution all over Australia. I was selling $10,000 worth of tires weekly.

Again, that wasn't important. Our wedding was. We settled on a date in December. Initially, there was a bit of disagreement with Roz's parents because we didn't want much fuss. We originally looked at something quite simple, getting hitched at the WA Marriage Registry. We didn't want all the bells and whistles of a formal church wedding. In the end there was a compromise.

On December 10, 1970, a Baptist minister we had found conducted the marriage ceremony in the living room of her parents' home in Alfred Cove, a suburb close to the Swan River. It was attended by family and a few close friends.

For our honeymoon a friend lent us an open-top Sunbeam sports car, which we drove to Jurien Bay, a pretty coastal town in the wheatbelt region of WA, 220 km north of Perth. We stopped at a village pub on the way to have a drink, and our newlywed situation must have been obvious. When we left, all the locals came out and cheered us on our way.

Honeymoon over, it was back to getting settled into married life. Roz was still at university. I continued to toil away with tires. We had rented a modest fibro house in North Freemantle, just a few minutes' drive from Beaurepaires.

We also had transport. I had the use 24/7 of a utility vehicle, or ute, albeit plastered with Beaurepaires' advertising. And we had a cute little kitten called Twiggy. Between work and university, we enjoyed life. Many an evening was spent sitting on the beach, watching the glorious sunsets over the Indian Ocean. During that Australian summer, there were days at the WACA, the Western Australian Cricket Association ground, to watch an Ashes Test Match between Australia and England. There were Australian Rules football (AFL) games to attend. Roz supported Swan Districts, a team whose colors were black-and-white vertical stripes.

Some weekends we would drive into the country surrounding Perth. WA at the time had a strange regulation covering the drinking of alcohol. On a Sunday, hotels were only allowed to sell drinks to 'travelers'.

You had to be a certain number of km away from home before you could imbibe. This meant that if you lived in Perth, you couldn't get a drink in a hotel there. The result: a mass exodus of people every weekend out of Perth to surrounding towns far enough away to qualify them as travelers.

I hate to think how many times we drove home 'over the limit'. It was a little bit like the old law, introduced during the First World War, partly as an attempt to improve public morality and partly as a war austerity measure, that had

Australian pubs close their public bars at 6 pm. A culture of heavy drinking developed during the time between finishing work at 5 pm and the mandatory closing time only an hour later.

Since most workers finished work at 5 pm, this fueled an hour-long speed-drinking session called 'the six o'clock swill', as men raced to get as drunk as possible in the limited time available. Thankfully, the various Australian states phased out the rule in the late 1930s and during the 1940s.

But on most Sundays, there was a family ritual. We'd go over to Alfred Cove where Roz's dad, in white singlet and shorts, would be lying on the floor watching an AFL match on the TV. Then a Sunday roast for dinner, followed by an evening playing the card game Five Hundred. They were fun-filled days. Roz's dad was an accountant, with a typical Australian dry sense of humor. He was one of the hardest-working people I ever knew. Hadn't taken a holiday for years and worked so hard he ended up buying the accounting firm he worked for. On weekday evenings he would disappear into his home office and continue his work.

6

On the move again, together this time

By the middle of 1971, our minds were turning to other possibilities. We had always talked about travel, and now we began planning how and when we should launch into what was essentially an Australian rite of passage.

It's almost a national custom for the country's youth. In their late teens or early twenties, they down tools or studies and head overseas for a year, usually to Britain. They mostly go to London and work as bartenders, waiters, waitresses, or any other job they can find, living in what has, over the years, become the Australian ghetto of Earl's Court. And during that time, they cross the Channel and do the rounds of Continental Europe.

While I wasn't yet a fully fledged Australian and still had a British passport, I was more than happy to join in. Besides, Ros had never been overseas, and, at some stage, I had to introduce my new wife to my parents in Edinburgh.

Late that year we flew out of Perth airport, first with Thai Airways International to Bangkok, where we spent a few days sightseeing, visiting a few magnificent gold-trimmed pagodas. Before traveling on, we bought a beautiful Thai Princess ring, studded with opals, for Roz – a little ironic since opals were decidedly an Australian gemstone. While they are found around the globe, such as in Mexico and the western US, 95% of the world's precious opal is mined in Australia, and it is the country's national gemstone.

In Bangkok, we boarded a Scandinavian Airlines (SAS) Boeing 707 to Copenhagen, with a refueling stop at Tashkent in the Soviet Union on the way. That in itself was an experience, still the era of the Cold War.

At Tashkent, all passengers had to disembark, handing over their passports to Russian security officials as they went. We were held in what can only be described as a pen, surrounded by high wire fencing. There was a single building with toilets, and as we stood waiting to reboard, music and propaganda was blasted at us from loudspeakers mounted on the fence. Some local people stared at us through the wire, as if we were aliens from another planet – a brief introduction to the world on the other side of what was then called the Iron Curtain.

From Copenhagen, after another round of sightseeing, we proceeded on a grand tour of Northern Europe, taking a ferry from Denmark to the Norwegian capital of Oslo, then heading by train to Stockholm, capital of Sweden. Tour over, we boarded a flight from Stockholm to London, then a trip on Scotland's famed locomotive, the Flying Scotsman, which whisked us north to Edinburgh's Waverley Station and my waiting parents.

Initially, Roz felt my mum was cold, unemotional, but that quickly changed because she was, in fact, a warm, kindly soul.

Dad was different. He was a perfectionist, who could do almost anything. He had a cupboard where he stored his tools, all in their rightful place and all perfectly maintained. As youngsters, we were forbidden to touch them. If we did, he would immediately spot where something was out of place, and we would be in trouble.

Something else seemed alien to Roz. This was a typical, old-fashioned, and traditional Scottish family. The man ruled the roost. Mum did all the washing and ironing. When Dad came home from work, he expected his slippers to be warm before the fire, and the evening meal to be ready. Even then, he would fiddle around in the kitchen, making sure everything was cooked properly. In other words, he could be very annoying at times.

Nevertheless, it was good to be back in Edinburgh after more than two years away, even though, to me, it wasn't home anymore. As 1971 became 1972, we spent New Year, or Hogmanay, in Edinburgh.

First, a dinner dance at a posh hotel in Princess Street, the city center's main thoroughfare. Then a bus back to Boswall and amazement by all when Roz removed uncomfortable high-heel shoes to walk the rest of the way to the house in bare feet … in the middle of a freezing winter.

And, as midnight came, a gathering of family and friends, someone playing Scottish tunes on an accordion as

Mum went through the Hogmanay rituals. Opening all the windows to let the old year out, and the front door to let the new year in. And, of course, drinks, nips of Scotch. We always had Scotch in the house, though the only time I ever saw Dad drink it was at New Year. I never saw him drunk.

With the New Year in, it was time to explore. We purchased a little green minivan, which we christened McTavish. First, it was around Scotland. North to Aberfeldy in Perthshire, where Roz saw her first snow, then Pitlochry and my relatives, before driving through the Cairngorm Mountains to Inverness and on to John O'Groats, the northernmost point on the Scottish Mainland. Round the barren top of Scotland and down the West Coast before returning to Edinburgh.

McTavish was to become a trusty friend. We parked by the roadside each night and slept in the back, cramped though it was. I can't remember it ever breaking down, even though it was to take us much further afield than around Scotland.

Other things had to be done. Roz still hadn't completed her university degree in Computer Science and had exams to sit. One of them she sat at St Andrews University while we were in Scotland. Later, she was to have a long and distinguished career lecturing Computer Science at Sydney's Macquarie University, where she also gained her Master of Science degree in 1996.

Looking back, it seems like a more-than ambitious plan, but we decided to set out for Europe. And not only

Europe – all the way to Istanbul. And not just Istanbul! We aimed to get there on a route that would take us, once again, behind the Iron Curtain. It involved some time arranging to get visas to some of the countries we would pass through, but having succeeded in doing that, we set off south. First to the south of England and a ferry to Belgium, then a drive through Germany to the Austrian capital of Vienna. It's a long time ago now, but the one thing I remember doing there was visiting the grave of composer Ludwig van Beethoven at the Währing cemetery, northwest of the city.

Next on the itinerary was Hungary and its capital Budapest, but before we got there, we experienced a shock. After crossing into Eastern Europe over the Austria–Hungary border, we parked in a lay-by at the side of the road, settling down for the night. Some hours later, in the dead of night, we were awakened by an earsplitting noise. All hell, it seemed, had broken loose. Tracer bullets climbed into the night sky and a convoy of army trucks roared past on the road. We had parked in the middle of a military exercise area.

Given that particular time in the history of Europe, with the Cold War alive and well, our first thought was: here we are, behind the Iron Curtain, in the middle of some military exercise, in a car with British number plates. They'll probably think we're British spies. We quickly packed up and set off along the road, keeping well behind the military convoy, which eventually turned off and disappeared to our left. No-one came chasing after us and all was well.

We drove through Hungary to Romania, and there is one thing I recall: the stark contrast between the West and the Communist East. Our route took us through kilometers of dark-soiled farmland, past villages that seemed like they hadn't changed since the 16th century, with peasants toiling in the fields.

Few cars were on the road, just locals on horse-drawn carts. We were forced to stop at one village because a line of men and women blocked the road. A house was on fire but with no fire engine they were passing buckets of water to the scene from a nearby stream.

From Romania's capital Bucharest we drove south to Bulgaria. The border between those two countries is the River Danube, a bridge linking the Rumanian town of Giurgiu with the Bulgarian town of Rousse. What puzzled me was why, as we crossed from one country to the other, there should be Kalashnikov-toting soldiers stationed every 100 yards along the bridge. After all, these were two communist nations, both part of the Soviet bloc. It was evidence of the iron grip the authorities in these nations held over their populace.

In Bulgaria we reached the Black Sea port of Burgas, where we camped on a beach. This time we weren't sleeping in the car, but in a tiny tent we had brought with us. From there, it was on to Turkey, crossing the border through a mountain pass, near the 1,031-meter-high Mount Mahya Dagi, and Istanbul.

After parking in the city, we were soon reminded that not all cultures are the same. As we left the car, it quickly became clear from the looks we got from passersby that something was amiss. Mini-skirts were not acceptable here. Roz had to get back to the car and change into jeans.

From Istanbul, we started on the long journey back to Scotland, first to Thessaloniki in Greece. At that Greek border, we were stopped and thoroughly checked over. The border officials even went through the car with a fine-tooth comb. They found a bag of something white and proceeded to smell and taste it. It was sugar. They wanted me to open the car bonnet so they could inspect the engine compartment. I couldn't get it open. Eventually they did. Apparently, this was a well-known route used by drug-smugglers.

After Greece, we traveled through Albania into what was then Yugoslavia, where we camped one evening in a field of grapevines. Later that night we were awakened by tapping on the car window. There stood a bearded giant wearing a sheepskin jacket, with a shotgun over his shoulder. He was guarding the grapes. Despite the obvious barrier of language, I managed to get across we were innocent tourists having a nap. He seemed friendly enough, despite the armament, and I cemented the deal by giving him a gift.

Earlier that day we had stopped at a village shop and purchased a liter bottle of what we thought was milk. It turned out to be yogurt and not very good for adding to coffee. I gave him the untouched bottle, and he seemed very pleased. And we went back to sleep secure in the knowledge that our slumber was being protected by a friendly bodyguard.

Today, the map of this part of Europe has changed dramatically. What was once Yugoslavia is now a group of individual nations: Montenegro, Kosovo, Serbia, and Bosnia and Herzegovina.

Back then, as you drove through Yugoslavia, the road ran through a mountain range and suddenly, lying beneath you, was an incredible panorama, with the blue waters of the Adriatic Sea as far as the eye could see. Then the road dropped in an endless series of hairpin bends, taking you to the stunning city of Dubrovnik. Now in Croatia, it is one of the most picturesque locations in the Balkans. The city is filled with limestone streets, baroque buildings, and big sea-facing walls, attracting tourists worldwide.

It was impossible to imagine then that years later, in late 1991, Dubrovnik would come under siege from the Yugoslav People's Army (JNA), attacking Croatian forces who were defending the city during the Croation War of Independence. The siege was accompanied by a Yugoslav Navy blockade and the city was bombarded, including the Old Town, a United Nations Educational, Scientific and Cultural Organization (UNESCO) World Heritage Site.

The bombardment provoked international condemnation and became a public relations disaster for Serbia and Montenegro, contributing to their diplomatic and economic isolation, as well as the international recognition of Croatia's independence. But future conflicts were far from our minds as we drove up the spectacular Adriatic coast, into Italy and on to Venice.

From there, we continued on through France, where one more tricky incident happened. On a motorway, as we approached Paris, Roz wanted to change her clothes into something more suited to the famed City of Love. She was doing that in the passenger seat when, suddenly, two French gendarmes on motorcycles pulled in ahead of us.

They dismounted and began walking back toward McTavish. Hurriedly, I leaped out of the car and walked toward them to stop them reaching the vehicle, where they would have seen a half-dressed woman in the front seat. It was a friendly encounter. Stopping on the motorway, they pointed out, was prohibited. But we were just foreign tourists, and it ended with an amiable directive to move on as quickly as possible. All blushes were avoided.

Soon, we were back across the Channel and heading, once again, to Scotland. It had been a memorable adventure. We weren't exactly rolling in cash. It had been a case of seeing western and eastern Europe on the cheap. Eating at restaurants or staying in hotels or motels had been out of the question. The food we ate was bought in local stores and cooked by the side of the road.

We have always said we'd love to do it again, but next time in luxury, staying at fancy hotels and eating in restaurants. Now, after a brief stay back in Edinburgh, we moved to London. It was to open a new chapter in my life, and I was, at last, to get back to having a typewriter in front of me.

7

The guerilla war years

Through all these years of involvement with tires, I never lost my ambition to get back into journalism. I knew in my heart that something would turn up. Somewhere … somehow …

In London, the world's journalistic mecca, I got a job with a small news agency. It wasn't Fleet Street, but it wasn't that far away. Unfortunately, it didn't turn out to be the big break I was hoping for. The agency, I soon discovered, survived by 'beating up' news stories. Its fare was drama, lewd court cases, and scandals. Even with coverage of more straightforward fare, such as a demonstration or protest, it pushed the boundaries. If there were 500 people involved, you were expected to write that there were more than a thousand.

All of this was aimed at making stories more attractive to the newspaper customers they supplied. In the end, the job didn't last for long. I wasn't their type of reporter, and their style of reporting wasn't my style of reporting. I had been trained in an old-school style, based on being accurate and honest in what you wrote.

Anyway, it wasn't long before I was up and running again. The *UK Press Gazette*, a British trade magazine dedicated to journalism and the press, first published in 1965, was the bible for any reporter looking for a new job. Its classified advertisement pages included ads from newspapers and media all over Britain and the world looking for new staff.

Immediately catching my eye was an ad from the Argus media group in South Africa, looking for a reporter to join the staff of one of its newspapers, the *Rhodesia Herald*, in Salisbury, the capital of Rhodesia.

I applied for and secured an interview with the manager of the Argus group's London Bureau. Along I went, armed with scrapbooks containing cuttings of stories I had written during my time with Scottish newspapers, hoping like hell he wouldn't notice the dates and realize there was a sizable gap in my journalistic career, but I needn't have worried. It turned out he was of Scottish descent, and we ended up having a friendly chat, mainly about Scotland and golf. He wasn't the least interested in my scrapbooks and ended the interview by simply asking, 'How soon can you go?'

Rhodesia? I really didn't know much about it, and I'd never imagined I'd go there, let alone work there. A little bit of research soon filled me in. This was a former part of the British Empire known as Southern Rhodesia. The name Rhodesia derived from Cecil John Rhodes, a British mining magnate and politician in Southern Africa who served as Prime Minister of the Cape Colony from 1890 to 1896. An ardent believer in British imperialism, Rhodes is notably quoted as having said, 'to be born English is to win first prize in the lottery of life'.

The rapid decolonization of Africa in the late 1950s and early 1960s alarmed a significant proportion of Southern Rhodesia's white population, and, to delay the transition to black majority rule, the predominantly white Southern Rhodesian government, under its Prime Minister, Ian Smith, issued its own Unilateral Declaration of Independence (UDI) from the United Kingdom on 11 November 1965.

The new nation, identified simply as Rhodesia, initially sought recognition as an autonomous realm within the Commonwealth of Nations but reconstituted itself as a republic in 1970. A landlocked nation, it was bordered by South Africa to the south, Botswana to the southwest, Zambia (formerly Northern Rhodesia) to the northwest, and Mozambique, a Portuguese province until 1975, to the east.

The UDI led to United Nations-imposed sanctions, though, as I was to learn, they didn't seem to have a lot of impact. For example, the British Royal Navy had warships patrolling the Mozambique Channel, purportedly to stop oil tankers offloading fuel at the Mozambique port of Beira, which would then be shipped overland to Rhodesia. In all the years I spent in Rhodesia, I never saw any sign of a petrol shortage.

Another major sanction-busting event happened in 1973, when three Boeing B720 jets suddenly appeared in Salisbury bedecked in the livery of Air Rhodesia. Their purchase was in breach of United Nations sanctions. How the deal was done was kept secret, but it later emerged they had originally belonged to America's Eastern Airlines, before being sold to a German holiday charter airline, Calair, and then a Swiss company called Jet Aviation. Rhodesia had secured a loan to purchase the aircraft from a Swiss and German bank in contravention of UN sanctions. Air Rhodesia concluded the purchase at secret negotiations in Basle, Switzerland, where the aircraft were parked. The airline's crew, who had undergone Boeing conversion courses, were sent to fetch them. They were flown first to a Portuguese military base, where the Air Rhodesia livery replaced the Calair markings, then on to Salisbury.

In the middle of 1972, when we headed for Rhodesia, there were certainly no direct flights between London and Salisbury. That would also have been a breach of United Nations sanctions. But it wasn't difficult. We simply flew aboard South African Airways to Johannesburg, with a refueling stop on the way at the Canary Islands. Then it was a one-hour flight north to the Rhodesian capital. The Herald had booked us into the aptly named Zebra Hotel until we found our own accommodation.

The *Rhodesia Herald* building overlooked Cecil Square, also named after Rhodes, a peaceful park awash with purple-draped jacaranda trees. It was a peace shattered late each night as the Herald's presses began to rumble, and the trucks rolled out loaded with copies of the next morning's edition.

My first story for the Herald was hardly a groundbreaking exclusive, but it was a defining moment. It was about a visit to the country by the Danish musical comedian, Victor Borge. When I finished writing, I handed my copy to the news editor and returned to my desk. There, I watched nervously as he read through it. When he had finished, he turned to his deputy and gave what was a definite nod of approval. Everything was going to be fine.

We settled down to life in what we quickly realized was a true hangover from colonial times. Everyone had a maid or a houseboy who did all the menial tasks like washing, ironing and generally keeping the house tidy. They were paid a pittance. Initially, we had an apartment in Fourth Avenue, close to the city center, without a maid. Later, when we moved into a two-storey garden flat in the suburb of Avondale, we did. I think we were generous. Others chided us for paying her too much.

At the same time, it was difficult to get used to the way things were. Rhodesia wasn't like South Africa under apartheid, where signs that declared 'Whites Only' or 'Blacks Only' were everywhere, and where interracial mixing was taboo.

In Rhodesia it was more subtle. Most Africans lived in Harare, which was pretty much a shanty town on Salisbury's outskirts. If you went into a shop with a queue of Africans, you would be served first. My insistence that I was happy to wait my turn was looked upon with some puzzlement.

Nor was there any problem with having gatherings or parties with people from both sides of the racial divide. One of my early stories at the Herald was to interview an African Rhodesian who worked for the United Nations in New York. He was home on leave, and after the interview invited me and my wife to join him and some of his friends for dinner at the Jameson Hotel, Salisbury's most upmarket establishment, which also overlooked Cecil Square.

At dinner, we were the only whites, dining with six Africans. I can only recall the name of one, Edison Sithole, a lawyer. The reason I remember is that a couple of years later he disappeared, never to be seen again, no doubt a victim of nationalist disagreements. Anyhow, during that dinner, my wife danced with one of the other guests, and it was clear from the disapproving glances of many of the white diners in the restaurant that this was not the done thing. For us these frowning glances flowed over us like water from a duck's back.

At work, for the time being at least, I was once again a general reporter covering anything and everything, even including reporting on weekend soccer matches. There were court cases aplenty, including murders. Rhodesia still had the death penalty. There were stories to write about these sanction-busting successes and reports on agriculture exports.

Tobacco was the country's main crop and, despite sanctions, remained a major export earner. The Portuguese authorities in neighboring Mozambique turned a blind eye to shipments going from Rhodesia to the port of Beira, as well as imports going the other way.

Then there was politics, which I increasingly began to cover. The Parliament of Rhodesia was organized in Westminster style, with two chambers, the Senate and the House of Assembly. The Senate had 23 members: ten white Rhodesians, ten African chiefs, and three persons appointed by the President of Rhodesia, Clifford Dupont.

The photo on my Argus Africa News Service press credentials. I thought I was bullet-proof and came through three guerilla conflicts without a scratch.

The president's post was almost entirely ceremonial, and the real power continued to be vested in the prime minister, Ian Smith. The House of Assembly had a popularly elected 66 members, 50 of them non-Africans and 16 of them African. Getting to know the politicians, including Ian Smith himself, and talking to them about the burning issues became a regular part of my beat.

Another regular task was interviewing the leaders of the African nationalist groups, which were increasingly beginning to make noises, demanding a bigger say in Rhodesia's future and campaigning for Black Rule. There were two nationalist groups, divided along tribal lines. Rhodesia was a typical product of British colonialism, an artificial territory that ignored traditional tribal borders. It ended up as a land populated by the Shona in the north and the Ndebele in the south. The Zimbabwe African People's Union (ZAPU), headed by Joshua Nkomo, consisted largely of Ndebele.

The Zimbabwe African National Union (ZANU), under Robert Mugabe, was Shona-predominant. Not surprisingly, while they both had the same endgame in mind, there were numerous disagreements about tactics, as well as tribalism and personality clashes. It all made for interesting reporting.

Mugabe had just been released after 10 years in prison, where he had earned several degrees by correspondence, one in Law. We attended parties he was at, where he presented a façade of amiability. He disappeared from the scene soon afterwards, having gone to Tanzania from where he would lead the armed struggle. Nevertheless, thinking back, it would have been difficult to predict he would become the tyrant that he did.

As has happened several times in my life, it turned out the timing of my African sojourn was perfect. No sooner had we settled in, and after a few months cementing my position as a reliable and professional reporter, fighting suddenly started.

On December 21, 1972, a gang of African terrorists attacked lonely Altena farm in the border area of Centenary,

200 km to the north-east of Salisbury. Terrorists blazed away at the homestead of farmer Marc de Borchgrave. The first casualty was his eight-year-old daughter Jane, who was wounded but recovered quickly in a Salisbury hospital.

Things quickly escalated. Two days later another farm, Whistlefield, came under rocket attack. The same day, the Rhodesian Army suffered its first casualty when a soldier was fatally wounded in a landmine explosion. As January 1973 arrived, incidents were occurring regularly. Two government land inspectors died in an ambush near Mount Darwin, in the north of the country.

Just days later, a farmer's wife, Ida Kleynhans, died in a hand grenade and automatic rifle attack on her husband's Centenary farm. Her husband, Chris, was wounded. By this time, I had become heavily involved in covering the conflict and was soon recognized as the Herald's official war correspondent. Not that it was straightforward.

The Rhodesian police Special Branch became a very important connection in my coverage of the war. Henry, of Danish background, and an Irishman we called Paddy, would phone and tip me off about attacks and other incidents. Then I would grab a Herald car, with its African driver, and a photographer to race to the scene.

On one occasion after driving along a dirt track, we arrived at a farm that had been attacked. Thirty minutes later, an army truck coming down the same track hit a landmine and was blown up. There, but for the grace of God, I could have gone.

Anyway, we had a cunning plan to deal with landmines, which were regularly planted by the terrorists. We figured if we drove fast enough, by the time it exploded, it would be behind us. Thankfully, the theory was never put to the test.

On another occasion, photographer Roger Bull and I went to Centenary, where we stayed with a farming family overnight to record how they were dealing with the situation. In an article I wrote later for the *Argus News*, an inhouse news-sheet for the Argus group, I commented on how covering the terrorist war being waged in Rhodesia's north-eastern border area could be confusing at times. I wrote:

> There's no front line really. No ranks of military men drawn up facing each other on clearly marked battlefields. Just the nagging thought that the terrorists could be in front of you, behind you, above you or even below you.

Going in and out of the troubled Centenary area in the daylight was one thing; spending the night there was a different thing altogether, I added. Then I went on:

> Night in Centenary can be unnerving. We drove to the farm well after dark. The narrow farm road twisted and turned through the rugged terrain. Dust from the track whirled everywhere and terrorists (we were quite sure) lurked behind every bush, tree, and blade of grass. The farm itself, we

were glad to note, sat atop a handy kopje (hill), looking impregnable. Security fencing stretched around the homestead, wired to warning buzzers inside the house.

The hardy farmer and his wife sat in a beautiful living room, furnished with expensive antiques. At his feet lay an automatic rifle and beside his wife a shotgun. Dinner was unbelievable. Sandbags covered the French doors, wire meshing on the windows. And by candlelight we ate a well-prepared meal with those ever-present rifles nearby. Our bedroom was the same. Wire mesh and steel plate covered the windows to deflect hand grenades and bullets. Our host knocked on the door and passed a rifle to Roger, a Beretta pistol for me. 'Just in case,' were his parting words.

Trips like that were part and parcel of what I was doing, and there were moments of comedy, depending on which side you were on. One farmer had a lucky escape as he drove away from his property, unaware a terrorist was lurking in the bushes by the roadside armed with a hand grenade. As the car approached, the insurgent pulled the pin from the grenade … and threw the pin, which bounced harmlessly off the vehicle's bonnet. The dumbfounded terrorist was left standing with live grenade in hand until the inevitable explosion and his untimely demise.

In the lobby of a hotel in Beira, Mozambique, where I slept through a grenade attack.

I made dozens of trips into the conflict zones in the north and northeast of Rhodesia, visiting farms that had been attacked. I watched Canberra bombers of the Rhodesian Air Force drop napalm on suspected terrorist hideouts, Hawker Hunter jets strafe fleeing terror groups, and I flew on the air force's ageing Dakota DC-4 transports, dropping supplies to units in the field.

You can imagine then that I was miffed when someone wrote a letter to the *Herald* that spoke of 'Journalists sitting back in the halls of safety in the heart of the city', while Rhodesia's youth were fighting – and dying – in the field. In response I wrote an article which said, in part:

> Not true. Rhodesia's terrorist struggle is being fought under a tight security screen. There are practical reasons for this. Security is as important in this struggle as the actual fighting. Yet despite this, journalists from Salisbury do risk their lives on trips to security areas. Since last December when the present wave of trouble

began, reporters have gone to Centenary, to Mount Darwin, Sipolilo, and even further into the north-east area. They have brought back reports of terrorist kidnappings, the struggle of the farmers in those hard-hit areas and chases by security forces against marauding terrorists. The farmers and security forces may carry guns. The journalists go unarmed. Driving over dusty roads, lonely farm tracks through thick bush where the terrorists could be hiding, where the landmine is an ever-present danger.

This was a dirty war. Europeans were not the only target. In the dead of night, the terrorists would creep into villages they suspected of cooperating with the Rhodesian authorities and kill the local headman. Or they would kill or maim African villagers, using pliers to rip off their ears or lips, or poke out their eyes.

Knowing who was who also proved difficult at times. Some Africans were farmhands by day, terrorists by night. Nor were all underhand practices on one side. While it was never spoken about publicly, it was known that Special Branch would take captive terrorists up in helicopters and threaten to throw them out if they didn't reveal where their arms cache was hidden or where their comrades were.

After a clash, security forces would fly us to the site of the skirmish and show off the bodies of the dead terrorists, stripped naked, their flesh ripped apart by machine gun fire.

I don't know why, but this never made me feel nauseous. It was part and parcel of a dirty war.

By the end of 1973, what had been tagged Rhodesia's Bush War had claimed the lives of 23 security force personnel, four South African policemen, who had been cooperating with Rhodesian forces near the northern border, and 15 civilians. Not all the civilian deaths were the result of terrorist action. Zambian troops fired across the Zambezi River at Victoria Falls, killing two young Canadian tourists. It was estimated 195 terrorists had also died. As well as this, 13 captured terrorists were hanged, and at least 58 tribesmen were convicted of giving aid to terrorists.

During all this tragedy, other developments were to change my future. In November 1973, Roz told me she was pregnant. Joy of joys! It hadn't been planned, but it was wonderful, one of the happiest days of my life. And around the same time a new career opportunity arrived.

Roger Bull, all set for the shooting to begin (see story below).

We slept–armed to the teeth

COVERING the sort of terrorist war being waged in the troubled north-eastern border area of Rhodesia at the moment tends to become a bit confusing at times, writes Tom Ballantyne.

There's no front line really. No ranks of military men drawn up facing each other on clearly marked battlefields. Just the nagging thought that the terrorists could be in front of you, behind you, above you or maybe even below you.

So when Herald photographer Roger Bull and I went into the war zone around Centenary recently for the umpteenth time we made doubly sure before leaving that our insurance cover was well in order.

We two intrepid journalists trekked off to the border area to find

TOM BALLANTYNE

candlelight we ate a well prepar meal with those ever present ri nearby.

We slept armed to the teeth in a remote farm, prepared for terrorist attack. Thankfully, the night passed without incident.

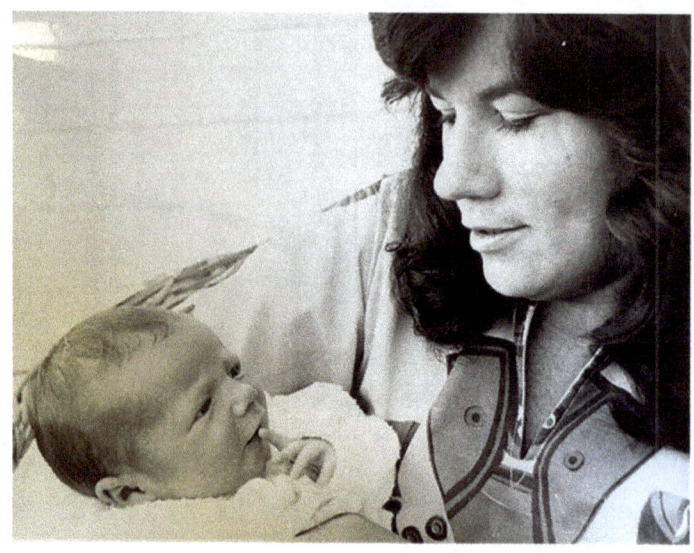

One of the happiest days of my life. Roz with our beautiful new daughter Tracey in Salisbury, Rhodesia.

Herald House, home of the Rhodesia Herald, in the early 1970s where my career really took off.

Certificate from the Rhodesian Defence Ministry exempting me from being called up into the military.

Covering the guerilla conflict in Rhodesia was a never-ending tale of sadness in a dirty war.

Black African troops of the Rhodesian army on patrol.

8

Wider horizons and more conflict

My coverage of the Rhodesian struggle for the Herald had attracted the attention of Wilf Nussey, Editor-in-Chief of the Argus Africa News Service (AANS). This news agency had been set up by the Argus group for a very specific reason. Reporters with South African passports were severely limited in their ability to travel around Black Africa, where many countries barred entry to anyone from the apartheid state.

AANS employed journalists with British, Australian, New Zealand, Canadian or other passports, who could travel freely to the many nations to the north of South Africa and provide coverage of events there for all the newspapers in the Argus group. This included *The Star* in Johannesburg, *The Cape Argus* in Cape Town, the *Durban Daily News* and *The Pretoria News*, in South Africa's capital.

Although the agency was headquartered in Johannesburg, I was to work from the Salisbury Bureau, so I didn't have far to go. The office was in the Herald building, directly above the newsroom where I had been working previously.

The Bureau Chief was a New Zealander, John Edlin, and the biggest change of all for me was that my 'patch' was undergoing a major expansion. Not only would I be covering events in Rhodesia, but also in Botswana to the west, Malawi and Zambia to the north, the Portuguese territories of Mozambique to the east, and Angola, which lay on Africa's west coast, north of Botswana. John and I would take turns traveling to the hot spots. Two weeks in Angola, then back home for a spell. A week or two in Mozambique, and back home again.

Travel to Zambia was via Malawi since there were no direct flights from Salisbury to Zambia's capital, Lusaka. Each trip was very different. Botswana was a quiet place, where little happened. Malawi was the same, a sort of neutral country happy to greet tourists from Rhodesia and South Africa.

Zambia, however, was unfriendly. It was where the ZAPU and ZANU guerillas had their camps, from which they crossed the Zambezi River to mount their attacks. They also had camps in Mozambique as well as southern Angola, from where they would infiltrate through Botswana into Rhodesia.

The Portuguese colonies were something else, and again, each was different in significant ways, although they were both in transition. A leftist military coup, called the Carnation Revolution, had overthrown Portugal's Estado

Novo dictatorship in Lisbon in April 1974, and the new regime immediately stopped all military action in the African colonies, declaring its intention to grant them independence without delay.

In Mozambique, there was a single guerilla group, Frelimo, the Frente de Libertação de Moçambique, or the Liberation Front of Mozambique, led by Samora Machel. Even before the Lisbon coup, Frelimo controlled much of the north of the country and governed many regions.

It didn't mean there was peace. There were still occasional attacks on white civilians and ambushes of cars. On my first visit to Beira for AANS, I woke up one morning and walked downstairs to find the hotel lobby in a mess. Someone had lobbed a hand grenade into the hotel during the night. Much to the amusement of my fellow journalists, I had slept on, oblivious to the sound of the explosion below. No-one was killed in the explosion, but a hotel receptionist on night duty was slightly wounded.

Angola was a different kettle of fish altogether. Here, the Portuguese military were strolling around Luanda, the capital, with flowers, usually carnations, dangling from the barrels of their rifles. For them, it had become *make peace, not war*. The problem was that others were not the least interested in making peace.

The Angolan War of Independence, or in Portuguese, Guerra de Independência de Angola, had started way back in 1961 as an uprising against the forced cultivation of cotton, but developed into a multi-faction struggle for control of the country. That fight with the Portuguese officially ended with the coup in Lisbon, but it left three nationalist groups and their military arms vying for power. In other words, the fight for freedom against the Portuguese very quickly turned into a civil war.

The three nationalist groups were the National Liberation Front of Angola (FNLA), the People's Movement of Liberation of Angola (MPLA), and the Union for the Total Independence of Angola (UNITA). The FNLA was led by Holden Roberto, a descendant of the old Kongo Royal House, who was born in northern Angola but had lived since his early childhood in the Belgian Congo. Its armed branch was the National Liberation Army of Angola (ELNA), and it was mainly backed by Congo/Zaire, where its troops were based and trained, and by Algeria, with some financial backing from the US. Even though the FNLA considered itself to be anti-communist, it received weapons from Eastern European countries.

The MPLA was headed by its president Agostinho Neto, a Portuguese-educated urban intellectual. It was mainly externally supported by the Soviet Union and Cuba. Its armed wing was the People's Army of Liberation of Angola (EPLA), which was mainly equipped with Soviet weapons received through Zambia.

UNITA was led by Jonas Savimbi, a dissident of FNLA who had clashed with Holden Roberto, accusing him of favoring the US and of following an imperialist policy. The armed wing was the Armed Forces of Liberation of Angola, and it got most of its backing from South Africa.

All of this made Angola a very dangerous place. My first visit was nerve-racking. You got there by flying to Johannesburg, then transferring to a South African Airways (SAA) service to Luanda. Even that could be hazardous. One SAA flight was fired on as it approached the Angolan capital, landing with a row of bullet holes in its tail.

On the ground, it was chaotic. We would hire a car with an Angolan driver, who would take us wherever we needed to go, making sure we had the large sign in the windscreen declaring PRESS. The various nationalist groups controlled different parts of the city, and there were roadblocks everywhere.

We also carried paper replicas of the flags of each of the warring groups. As you approached a roadblock, you had to quickly decide whether it was manned by FNLA, MPLA or UNITA, grab their flag, and slap it onto the windscreen. Pick the wrong flag and you were more than likely going to end up at the wrong end of a salvo from a Kalashnikov.

These roadblocks were manned by fighters, many of whom were little more than kids – teenagers, some as young as 13 or 14. And trigger-happy. We always carried a Polaroid camera with us because if you could take their picture and give them an instant snap, they were as happy as children in a toy shop.

There were other risks. A colleague, an American television film cameraman, was taken into custody by one of the groups and accused of being a CIA spy. He was tortured, some of his nails pulled out, before finally being released so he could leave the country.

Unlike Rhodesia, Portugal's military were happy to let us accompany them on patrols. One night in Luanda, moving slowly through the suburbs with a couple of armored cars, we came to a sudden halt. Ahead of us, a fierce firefight was underway between two guerilla groups, one on each side of the road. The Portuguese were supposed to be playing some sort of peacekeeping role, keeping the warring factions apart, but there was no way they were going to get involved in this skirmish.

At one point, a couple of stray bullets pinged off the side of our armored car. The young lieutenant in charge of the patrol simply turned to me, shrugged, and declared, 'No worry. Accident.' So, we sat there for twenty minutes until the noise came to an end, and the night fell silent before proceeding on our merry way.

In Angola I also had to travel to the south of the country, UNITA's stronghold, but where there were also training camps for South African freedom fighters. I have to say I had a lot of sympathy for these young men as they spoke of how they were preparing for armed struggle to free their homeland. After all, they were refugees from a country in which they were treated as slaves, barred from interracial social contact, paid a pittance for the work they did, and had no say in their future. Their leader, Nelson Mandela, at that time had been imprisoned for more than a decade.

On one visit to head office in Johannesburg, the taxi I took from the airport into town stopped at traffic lights. An African messenger on a motorbike pulled up alongside us, and the taxi driver turned and looked at him.

'Have you ever seen anything that looks more like a monkey in your life?' he asked. I was appalled, but it was just one example of the bigotry and racism that was part and parcel of the apartheid regime. Something that I, and much of the rest of the world, viewed as abhorrent.

In the middle of this chaos, joy arrived in our life. Our daughter was born on July 11, 1974. We christened her Tracey Nicolle, and, like all new parents, thought she was the most beautiful baby in the world. And she was. Her arrival wasn't without a little bit of farce. I had been away on a one-day assignment to the town of Umtali, on the border with Mozambique, where Prime Minister Ian Smith was delivering a speech.

I returned well after midnight to find my wife apparently having labor pains – *definitely* having labor pains. What to do? We didn't have a telephone in the house, so I went out to find a public phone to call the hospital. Every phone I found was out of order and, eventually, I ended up at the hospital.

'I think you'd better go back and get her,' said the nurse, a wry smile on her face at this guy who had rolled up at maternity without his very pregnant wife.

They were crazy times, and we did some crazy things. We had purchased a little second-hand, two-seater sports car, a bug-eyed, blue Austin Healey Sprite. Initially, it had no roof, so we were open to the vagaries of the weather. However, Roz's parents in Australia managed to get a canvas soft top and sent it to us, so we were eventually protected from the rain.

A break from conflict. Roz with our little blue bug-eyed Austin Healey Sprite on the Mozambique coast, somewhere between Beira and Laurenco Marques. Guerilla-cum-Freedom Fighter threats or not, you just had to have a break.

So, when I was tipped off terrorists had raided a remote mission school in the northeast and kidnapped dozens of schoolchildren, I had to drive to the scene. These kidnappings were relatively common. The kids were marched across the border into Mozambique, to be eventually trained as child soldiers. Rhodesian units were on their trail, even crossing into Mozambique to rescue them.

What was crazy about this assignment? I decided to take my wife and baby daughter with me. The drive to the mission in our little sports car was uneventful, but by the time I had finished interviewing the priests and some children who had escaped the kidnappings by hiding in nearby bush, it was dusk. The light was fading fast, and we were driving along narrow, dusty, twisting tracks with thick bush on either side in country where terrorists were known to be active and where landmines were an ever-present danger. At one stage we took a wrong turn, got lost, and had to backtrack. It was spine-chillingly scary.

Although we eventually made it home safely, looking back, even years later, it horrifies me to think what could have happened. It was stupid. I had treated it like a day out with the family and put the lives of my wife and child at risk.

On another occasion, a Special Branch tip that terrorists were planning a mortar attack on Umtali, firing from across the border in Mozambique, had me on the way, once again with wife and daughter. Again, nothing happened but taking your nearest and dearest into possible risk was another example of a stupid decision.

As it happened, in October 1976, when I was safely ensconced back in Australia, my old boss Wilf Nussey wrote telling me head office had given its reporters in Salisbury permission to carry a 12-bore shotgun on trips to eastern Rhodesia. He added:

> Then there's the guerilla war stepping up fast, with Alex Morrowsmith, your successor, sitting at a top floor window of the Cecil (Hotel) in Umtali watching the mortar bombs fall all over the place in town. Quite a time. Alex, as a former Black Watch officer and a very tough little gorbals (Glasgow) man, loves it. His nickname, by the way, is the Tartan Dwarf or the Poisoned Dwarf (depending on your standing with him) and he has a reputation of breaking up pubs after one drink over the mark. But a delightful guy withal.

It seems that the tip I had from Special Branch about a mortar attack on Umtali was correct, just a couple of years premature.

But there were lighter moments. On one foray into Mozambique, I was at Tete, a town in the far north of the country. It was a Frelimo stronghold, but the freedom fighters were welcoming to international media. They were happy to pose for photographs with their Soviet-supplied Kalashnikovs and rocket-propeled grenade (RPG) launchers. After all, they knew victory was within their grasp.

As we were leaving town, I asked our driver to stop at a local supermarket. While sanctions weren't having much impact in Rhodesia, one thing in short supply was baby food. I pretty-much swept the store's shelves clean of as much baby food as I could find. Going back through border control at Umtali, the customs officer opened the boot of our car to be greeted with the sight of dozens of little jars of baby food. He smiled and closed the boot. After all, this was probably my one and only venture into sanction-busting.

There were other not-so-dangerous experiences. I was going to Zambia, flying via Blantyre in Malawi. Unfortunately, my flight from Salisbury was delayed, and by the time I arrived in Blantyre, where my stop was supposed to have been a brief transit, the Lusaka flight had already gone. I had to stay in Blantyre for the night and catch the Lusaka service the next day.

The issue was that Malawi is an extremely conservative country with strict rules. For example, women were not allowed to wear mini-skirts. Men were not allowed to have long hair, and my hair was decidedly long at the back, well over collar length. So, before I was allowed to enter the country, I was marched into an airport toilet by a customs officer, who quickly hacked off the offending blonde locks. Not pretty, but then hair would eventually grow back.

Something about Zambia also became familiar. Every time you were sitting in a bar having a drink, an Irishman would appear and strike up a conversation, politely inquiring who you were, where you had come from, why you were visiting, and what you would be doing. This, you could be certain, was a member of the Zambian Special Branch, which was mostly staffed by Irish policemen. Why the Irish were so involved in policing in darkest Africa I never quite worked out.

The nationalist leaders in Zambia were mostly happy to talk to international media. They were zealous, clearly dedicated to their goal of Black majority rule in Rhodesia. They insisted conflict was the only way and that achieving their aim was impossible through peaceful means. They argued that attacks and killing of white 'colonialists' was totally justified. What they did vehemently refute was any suggestion that their freedom fighters were murdering and torturing African villagers, even though I had personally seen evidence of it myself.

In Mozambique, despite the April 1974 coup in Lisbon, Frelimo leader Machel was still refusing to give the Portuguese the ceasefire they wanted. He declared that if there was no commitment to Mozambican independence, the conflict would continue. Frelimo reopened its front in Zambezia province and stepped up operations throughout the war zone.

There was little resistance. Following the collapse of the Portuguese government, rank-and-file Portuguese soldiers saw little point in continuing to fight, preferring to stay in their barracks. Finally, after talks in Lusaka on September 7, an agreement was signed that full power would be transferred to Frelimo with the date for independence set for June 25, 1975.

For a time Machel continued to run Frelimo from Tanzania, but he returned home triumphantly in a journey 'from the Rovuma to the Maputo' – the rivers marking the northern and southern boundaries of the country – in which he addressed rallies in every major population center in the country. I flew to the capital, Lourenco Marques, to cover his arrival there. At a reception, a long queue of people lined up to congratulate him and shake his hand. I was one of them.

On June 25, 1975, Machel proclaimed 'the total and complete independence of Mozambique and its constitution into the People's Republic of Mozambique'. This, he said, would be:

> ... a state of People's Democracy, in which, under the leadership of the worker-peasant alliance, all patriotic strata commit themselves to the destruction of the sequels of colonialism, and to annihilate the system of exploitation of man by man.

His presidency was to be relatively short, just ten years. On October 19, 1986, after attending a summit in

Zambia, the plane carrying him back to Maputo crashed just inside the South African border. Machel and 33 others died, although nine people sitting at the back of the plane survived. An official investigation put the accident down to pilot error by the aircraft's Soviet crew.

But years later, in 2007, Jacinto Veloso, one of Machel's most unconditional supporters within Frelimo, claimed in his memoirs that the Soviet ambassador to Mozambique had asked Machel for an audience to convey the USSR's concern about Mozambique's apparent 'sliding away' toward the West, to which Machel supposedly replied 'Vai à merda!' (Go to hell!) Having then commanded the interpreter to translate, he left the room. Convinced that Machel had irrevocably moved away from their orbit, the Soviets allegedly did not hesitate to sacrifice the pilot and the whole crew of their own plane.

But back in 1974, as the festive season approached, we decided it was time for a serious break. We flew to Johannesburg and boarded a South African Airways jet bound for Perth to spend Christmas with Roz's parents and for them to get to know their new granddaughter. It was the breath of fresh air we needed.

Back in Southern Africa, my life was one of strong contrasts. In Salisbury we enjoyed parties, socializing with friends, weekend picnics, and poolside barbecues. But through my work, I was confronted daily by the grim news of conflict and developments in the bush war and in my trips in and out of Mozambique and Angola. In Perth, we could focus on peace and relaxation and the joys of family, Christmas, and New Year.

In Rhodesia the conflict was also worsening, and the government was calling up every able-bodied man, up to and including 50-year-olds. It was still a shock when a letter arrived ordering Rifleman T Ballantyne, number 95049, to report for duty.

This won't do, I thought. I immediately wrote back seeking an exemption on the grounds that I was a foreign correspondent, and that part of my job involved going to Zambia, Mozambique, and Angola, where I would be interviewing nationalists, even some terrorists. Being identified as a member of the Rhodesian military would put me in even greater danger.

Thankfully, the exemption certificate was issued, and I could breathe a sigh of relief. The speed with which it was granted was due to intervention by my Special Branch buddies, who saw me as more important as a source of information after my various visits outside Rhodesia than as someone slogging a rifle through the bush.

After every trip I made, the first thing would be a phone call from Henry or Paddy, asking me to come for a cup of coffee. They were pumping me for information. I didn't feel like a spy. Certainly, I didn't tell them everything, and what I did tell them, I was going to be writing for public consumption anyway.

There were very few breaks from covering the various conflicts, although something did occur that was totally different. We were tipped off that film stars Elizabeth Taylor and Richard Burton, who had divorced a year earlier, were remarrying, this time at the Chobe National Game Reserve in Botswana. In those days, money was no problem. I hired a light aircraft to fly there with a photographer.

By the time we got to the village of Kasane, the marriage had already taken place, and Burton and Taylor were ensconced in a secluded chalet in the Chobe Reserve, refusing to see or speak to the media. We did interview the official who had performed the service.

Ambrose Masalila, the District Commissioner in Kasane, described how the couple had been married by special license a few days earlier in a simple ceremony lasting 20 minutes. The couple had exchanged ivory wedding rings, and the only witnesses, in the small, dark brick commissioner's office, were two white workmen from the game park. Afterwards they drove to the banks of the Chobe River and toasted each other with champagne while two hippos and a rhino looked on. Sadly, this wedding was also doomed to failure. They divorced for a second time less than a year later.

Back in Angola, things were getting even more serious. In early November 1975, a Cuban military force flew into Luanda to support the MPLA. Performed under the tag Operation Carlota, there were 100 specialists and 88 men of Cuba's elite special forces.

At the same time, South Africa decided to flex its muscles. In what it called Operation Savannah, a military incursion began deep into Angola with the objective of driving the MPLA, Soviet, and Cuban forces out of southern Angola to strengthen the position of UNITA, the main opponent of the MPLA and an ally of South Africa.

I headed south from Luanda by car to meet the advancing column, but we were quickly stopped at an MPLA roadblock where they roughly told us to turn round, go back to Luanda and keep our noses out of it. Anyhow, the venture failed, and the South African forces were compelled to withdraw due to MPLA, Cuban, and Soviet pressure.

Back in Luanda, things were getting edgier. MPLA fighters were increasingly knocking on hotel doors in the middle of the night and taking individual journalists away for 'questioning'. We all believed it was only a matter of time before it would be our turn, so, with great relief, my stint in Angola came to an end, and I boarded the flight back to Johannesburg and on to Salisbury.

Through 1975, the situation in Rhodesia worsened. Incidents were no longer confined to the remote bush. There were attacks within Salisbury, including hand grenades being thrown into stores and cafes.

This, we finally decided, was no place to bring up a child. I handed in my resignation from AANS, and we prepared for a return to Australia. Probably just as well. In March 1976, when we were already back in Australia, Machel's government implemented United Nations sanctions against the Smith government and closed the borders with Rhodesia.

Previously, ZANU guerillas had operated from Frelimo-held areas in Tete province into northern areas of Rhodesia. Now, the entire length of the border was available for nationalist incursions and the attacks escalated.

Africa had been exciting. I had covered conflicts and experienced dangerous and risky moments, traveling into areas of known terrorist activity, or dealing with teenage freedom fighters armed to the teeth at roadblocks. But I'm not even sure I could call myself a REAL war correspondent.

My experiences were nothing like the reporters who covered more traditional conflicts, such as America's invasion of Iraq, or the Ukraine where on the front line they must live with constant artillery bombardments and incoming missile attacks and where armies fought each other from the trenches. Nevertheless, whether it's a shadowy guerilla war or open battle between two foes, there is always a measure of luck involved whether you survive or not.

In my twenties in Africa, I probably thought I was bulletproof, and those other reporters probably thought the same. As it turned out, I was.

9

Down Under, part two

On February 27, 1976, we left Salisbury by train, seen off by friends, work colleagues, and Henry and Paddy from Special Branch. I wasn't sure whether that was a mark of friendship or whether they were just there to make sure I was really going. I like to think the former since our relationship had always been businesslike and amiable, and we had socialized many times in the Quill Club, where Salisbury-based foreign journalists gathered. Paddy was still on the train farewelling us when it began to pull out of the station, and he had to dash to the door and leap out onto the platform.

The rail journey took us south to Bulawayo, Rhodesia's second largest city, then west, crossing the Zambezi at Victoria Falls, through Botswana to enter South Africa at Mafeking and on to Johannesburg. There, I left the train with Tracey, now more than 18 months old, while Roz went on to the port of Durban to have a couple of quiet days by herself. Even though she was still a baby, Tracey had her own Rhodesian passport, although we quickly also had her registered as an Australian citizen.

I had stopped at Johannesburg to make a short detour to the Australian Embassy in Pretoria. Still a British passport-holder, I had to get a new visa to re-enter Australia. To do that I had to have a certificate from the Rhodesian police certifying that 'there are no convictions for any crime recorded in Rhodesia, against Thomas Ballantyne'. Duly done. I also had to attend an in-person interview with a consular official at the embassy. Duly done. The visa was issued on March 1, and I proceeded, with Tracey in tow, to rejoin Roz in Durban.

On March 2, we exited South Africa, boarding the Lloyd Triestino liner *Galileo Galilei* for the ten-day cruise across the Indian Ocean to the Port of Freemantle in WA. It was a migrant ship, carrying mostly Italian immigrants from Europe heading for a new life in Australia.

The crossing was smooth, except for one bit of drama with Tracey. She fell out of bed, and as she was sleeping on the top bunk in our cabin, it wasn't a short plunge to the floor. Checked over by the ship's doctor, she was declared OK, except for a large bump on her forehead. We landed at Freemantle on March 12.

It was wonderful being back in Australia. We were in a place where there was no conflict, and Tracey was having more time being spoiled by her grandparents. For me, however, was the important matter of finding a new job. I was now armed with a glowing reference from my AANS boss, Wilf Nussey, which declared:

> Tom Ballantyne has worked for this organisation
> for two years and has consistently met the high

standards demanded for objectivity and accuracy, often under much difficulty in the fast-shifting African political scene. He has been based in Salisbury, Rhodesia, where he has concentrated on covering the internal guerilla warfare and its politics, as well as the conflicts in Angola and Mozambique, with such efficiency that he has kept steadily ahead of our opposition. He is a willing and hard worker and a good companion, and I have no hesitation in recommending him for any newsgathering post.

Once again, no vacancies at any of Perth's newspapers, so I wrote to newspapers on the east coast, in Melbourne, Sydney, and Brisbane. Most of the replies were disappointing, but one offered a glimmer of hope. It was from *The Sydney Morning Herald*, commonly known as the SMH, Australia's premier daily newspaper. The News Editor, Alan Dobbyn, wrote:

> Dear Mr. Ballantyne, Thank you for your letter. I am sorry to tell you that the prospect of a suitable vacancy on the Herald is not bright at present. However, I would be pleased to have a talk with you on your arrival in Sydney. If you phone my secretary, Miss Fenton, she will arrange a time.

An interview was better than nothing. So we set out for Sydney. My father-in-law gave us his old Holden station wagon, and we were Nullarbor bound – a 3,000-km drive where we negotiated that long unpaved stretch of highway, where the dust was so fine that when you opened a tightly zipped suitcase, the contents were still covered in red dust.

In Sydney, we stayed with friends for a while before renting a flat in Campsie, an inner-city suburb, mainly populated by Lebanese people, and I phoned Miss Fenton to arrange that interview with Alan Dobbyn.

My timing was perfect. The SMH was the sort of place that if you got a job, it was pretty much yours for as long as you wished. Very few people were dismissed. As it happened this time, a young Canadian reporter – his bad luck and my good fortune – had somehow got himself into the editor's bad books and had been sacked. There was a vacancy. Interview over, I was told I'd get a written decision on whether I had the job within a few days.

When it came it was another of those Eureka moments:

> Dear Mr. Ballantyne, We are now able to offer you a position as a B-grade journalist. There would be a three-month period of probation before confirmation of your appointment, a condition which applies to all engagements of journalists at the Herald. I should be grateful for your written acceptance and advice of the day on which you can begin duty.

That was easy: as soon as you want. The probationary period didn't bother me. After three grueling years in

Africa, I was super confident of my journalistic abilities. The three months passed quickly, and on August 9, 1976, an internal memorandum lobbed onto my desk from News Editor Alan Dobbyn, copy to Chief of Staff (CoS) Ian Frykberg, confirming that I had satisfactorily completed my probationary period and confirming my appointment to the Herald staff.

The SMH building was on Broadway, a stone's throw from Sydney's central business district. Owned by the John Fairfax newspaper group, it not only housed the SMH, but also the *Australian Financial Review* and an evening newspaper, *The Sun*, which ceased publication in 1988.

The newsroom was the same as that one I had first experienced in Edinburgh as a youngster. The constant click-clack of typewriters as reporters wrote their stories. The pinging of bells as they hit the new paragraph key. The haze in parts of the room. Smoking was still normal and accepted in the office.

Looking back, I can't say those early months at the SMH were thrilling. As a general reporter and a new member of staff, I was mostly assigned run-of-the-mill stories: the day-to-day bits and pieces that filled the gaps between major stories.

There would be periods in the police rounds room, listening in to the chatter on the police radio wavelength. Rushing out to report on car accidents. Then a few weeks at various courts, covering trials. Or down at State Parliament doing the legwork for the senior political reporters. But for me, that was fine. It was really all about cementing my position and working toward bigger things.

There was a fleet of radio cars with drivers who would take you out to assignments. The radios were essential – no mobile phones in those days. So, the radio allowed you to call back into the office and update the CoS or his deputy on how your story was developing. If you were close enough and had time, you would get back to the newsroom and type your story there. If you were too far away, you would have to find a public phone box and call in to a copytaker, who would type your story out as you dictated it. This was frequently a challenge for me as one or two of the copytakers had a bit of an issue with my Scottish accent. It meant I often had to repeat words or slowly spell them out to be sure they were being typed accurately.

In those days, bylines were restricted to a chosen few, the senior political reporters, the specialists covering subjects such as health, the environment, and industrial relations. My copy would have nothing on it at all, or a simple 'By a Herald Reporter'.

I now have no idea why, but my first byline with the SMH was on a rather innocuous piece about citizens' band radio (CB), mainly used by truck drivers or four-wheel drive enthusiasts going out into the bush. My second was a little more substantial, although hardly exclusive.

Under the headline 'Behind the Jindivik – 25 years and $56m' it began:

Twenty-five years ago today a small, slim-bodied jet aircraft roared into the blue Australian sky from the experimental rocket range at Woomera in South Australia. At 11 am this morning one of the successors of that plane, a Royal Australian Navy Jindivik target aircraft, will make a historic 45-minute flight from the Jervis Bay missile range in NSW to mark the 25th anniversary of that first pilotless flight. On August 29, 1952, the Jindivik – an Aboriginal word meaning 'hunted one' – successfully completed its first remote-controlled flight.

But that story did mark the beginning of a new phase in my SMH career. Possibly because of my experience in Africa, I was more and more being assigned to stories involving Australia's armed forces. Happily, for me, this wasn't going to involve any real combat, but it did have its moments.

The Royal Australian Air Force (RAAF) at one stage hosted a large group of journalists, flying us in one of their Hercules transport planes from their Richmond base outside Sydney to RAAF Base Edinburgh near Adelaide in SA. The purpose was to show off their fleet of Lockheed Orion aircraft, used for maritime reconnaissance around Australia's coast.

All of that went smoothly, but on the return flight, the plane suddenly hit an air pocket, plunging 1000 meters in seconds. It was both heart-stopping and comical. A RAAF airman had been emptying the latrine, and its contents ended up dripping from the top of his head.

When it was over, a Royal Australian Navy officer yelled out, 'That's exactly why you should fly Navy'.

But there was a serious side. I was OK, having had my seatbelt fastened. A few did not. They had hit the roof and crashed back down onto the steel floor of the cabin. One journalist suffered spinal injuries, and several others were battered and bruised. We had to make an emergency landing in Canberra so that the injured could be rushed to hospital.

A few weeks later, I was on a flight to Darwin, where I was to board a Royal Australian Navy patrol boat for a five-day cruise along the remote coastline of northern Australia. Its task was to seek out drug-smugglers or people-smugglers, who brought illegal immigrants, mainly from Indonesia in rickety boats. Often the only evidence of a landing would be footprints in the sand along the many kilometers of deserted beach. The navy would contact police ashore, who would go and investigate.

The skies above were also being patrolled by RAAF reconnaissance Orions, looking for suspicious vessels and directing the navy patrol toward them. A boarding party would search the boat for any evidence of drugs or illegal immigrants.

Another target was illegal fishing inside Australia's international waters. The navy was particularly keen to catch anyone who was shark-finning. There was a big demand and good profits for shark fins for shark-fin soup and traditional cures, particularly in China. Shark-finning involved removing fins and throwing the rest of the shark back into the ocean. They were often still alive, but without fins couldn't swim effectively, sinking to the bottom and dying of suffocation or being eaten by other predators.

I wasn't, by any means, an official defense correspondent, and other assignments meant there was a lot of variety.

On October 1977, I got my first bylined front-page lead. It was an exclusive interview with two Australian teachers, Geoffrey Sands and Barry Aslett, who had been aboard a Japan Airlines Douglas DC 8 jet when it was hijacked by Japanese Red Army terrorists. The plane was flying from Paris to Tokyo with a stopover in Bombay (now Mumbai), India. Shortly after taking off from Bombay's Santa Cruz International Airport, the five terrorists leaped from their seats waving guns and grenades and took control.

The pilot was ordered to take the plane to Dacca, capital of Bangladesh, where the hijackers planned to open negotiations aimed at having five of their comrades released from prison in Japan. Unfortunately, there were problems in Dacca: an attempted coup was underway, the Bangladesh Air Force had mutinied, and the terrorists couldn't find anyone to negotiate with. They flew on to Kuwait, by which time the Japanese Government had agreed to their demands, releasing the prisoners. The two Australians were among a group of passengers released at Kuwait, where I tracked them down at the British Embassy.

In a lengthy phone interview, they told me how they had feared for their lives. The terrorists had planted plastic explosives all around the aircraft and threatened to blow the plane up if there was a rescue attempt. Yet despite this, the two said the hijackers were generally courteous, addressing passengers as 'ladies and gentlemen'. The hijackers hadn't released all their hostages at Kuwait. They flew on to Damascus, where more were released. Finally, the aircraft was flown to Algeria, where it was impounded by authorities, and the remaining hostages were freed.

For a change of pace, the following month I was in Ballina, 740 km north of Sydney, for the arrival of 54-year-old grandmother Anne Gash, who was completing a solo round-the-world voyage in her tiny 8.3-m sloop *Llimo*. She left Sydney in July 1975, sailing via Cape Town to England, then across the Atlantic, through the Panama Canal, across the Pacific, and back to Australia, where she arrived on November 18, 1977.

While Africa was now part of my history, it was difficult not to see what was going on there. The SMH foreign pages carried news from Rhodesia nearly every day as the conflict there worsened. In August 1977, we carried a story about a Woolworths store in Salisbury being bombed by nationalist guerillas. Eleven civilians were killed and 76 were injured. Of those killed, eight were Black Rhodesians, including two pregnant women and a young boy, and three were whites, members of a single family. It confirmed our decision to leave had been the right one.

At the SMH, as Christmas approached, it was all about casinos. They were banned in New South Wales (NSW), but illegal casinos were operating all over Sydney, describing themselves as private clubs. Everyone knew about them, but the police simply ignored them.

So, when State Premier Neville Wran announced he had decided to have them closed, we expected some action. I was sent out to investigate. The announcement, it appeared, had caused hardly a ripple. My report said five of the city's main illegal casinos were operating as normal.

> At one of the city's best known illegal gambling spots, the Goulburn Club in Goulburn Street, a club official stood at the door as patrons entered and left freely. He told me the manager 'was not in, and that's the truth'. Through the foyer I could see the roulette wheels spinning and cards being dealt. About 20 customers were in the club. At the Forbes Club in Forbes Street, Woolloomooloo, the door was closed, and two short-sleeved attendants stood outside. Through a glass panel brightly lit chandeliers were clearly visible, and members were ushered inside quickly. A sign on the wall outside the club read Members Only. In Oxford Street, Bondi Junction, the Telford Club was also operating as usual. An official said there was 'no way' I could speak to the manager. Within five minutes' walk

of the Forbes Club, the Palace Club in Rockwell Crescent – a secluded dead-end street in Potts Point – showed no sign of reaction to the threat of closure. Once again, the manager was 'away'.

There was no sign of a single policeman anywhere, nor was there to be in future. The clubs simply kept operating with little or no interference from the authorities.

The festive season over, my new year began with an upgrade. I was now an A-grade journalist and was soon to be on the move again. The top brass at the Herald had something in mind for me.

10

Victoria beckons

In early 1978 I was appointed Melbourne Bureau Chief. Once again, we packed the car, this time driving south to the Victorian capital. In Melbourne, you would have thought the *Herald* Bureau would have been in the premises of *The Age*, Victoria's premier newspaper. Like the *Herald*, it was owned by the Fairfax Group. Instead, the office was in the publishing headquarters of the *Herald and Weekly Times* in Flinders Steet. It was owned by a major Fairfax rival, Rupert Murdoch's News Corporation. But all the Australian state capital city newspapers were here: *The West Australian*, the *Adelaide Advertiser*, Brisbane's *Courier-Mail*, and the *Hobart Mercury*.

It was a tight community of non-Victorians, and I soon learned everyone helped each other out. If someone missed a story, the others would pass on the information they needed, unless you were working on an exclusive, of course. As it was with the AANS bureau in Salisbury, The Herald Bureau in Melbourne was staffed by two reporters, me and a cadet. The cadet did all the routine assignments. As bureau chief, of course, I had all the plum jobs.

Melbourne was a rich source of news, from major industrial disputes to politics and crime. Particularly crime. And, just a few weeks after arriving, I was reporting on a huge robbery.

On St Patrick's Day, March 17, I had been in the penthouse suite at the exclusive, 5-star Hotel Windsor, interviewing the Prime Minister of the Cook Islands, Sir Albert Henry.

He had called an election and was in Melbourne touting for votes among the large Cook Island community living in the city. I say *touting*. He had a suitcase full of cash that he was handing out to all and sundry. In other words, he was buying votes. Henry won the election, but his victory soon turned sour. The result was overturned when a judge found he had used government money to fly hundreds of supporters from New Zealand to the Cook Islands to vote.

As I left that interview, word got to me that there had been a major robbery in an office building just a couple of blocks away. It turned out this wasn't just a robbery, but a triple murder. The heist had taken place on the eighth floor of the Manchester Unity building, a massive Gothic structure which housed the offices of several diamond merchants. The thief, or thieves, had tied the hands of three jewelers behind their backs, forced them to lie on the ground, then shot each of them, execution style, in the back of the head with a .22 rifle. Some $50,000 worth of diamonds had been stolen.

This story made front-page headlines in newspapers all over Australia, including the SMH. The hunt for the perpetrators went on for months. No-one was ever charged with the crime, although police did have a prime suspect, a serial killer called Alex Tsakmakis, but leads failed to produce any solid evidence.

Perhaps in a case of justice prevailing, Tsakmakis was later sentenced to life for a separate murder and armed robbery, and he himself was murdered in 1988 by a fellow inmate at Melbourne's Pentridge Prison, who bashed his head in with a pillowcase packed with gym weights. To this day, the murders of the three jewelers remain on Victorian police files as unsolved.

The Manchester Unity murders were by no means an isolated case. At the end of March, I was writing that in the first three months of the year, there had been 15 callous, cold-blooded, and gruesome murders in Victoria. Eight of them remained unsolved.

Three days after the three jewel merchants were murdered, the body of a 12-year-old Melbourne schoolgirl was found near Wandong, 55 km north of Melbourne. She had been raped and brutally bashed to death.

Two days later came the grisly find of the 'body in the box'. The legs of a female victim were crammed into a cardboard carton and the torso in a canvas bag was recovered nearby.

Police were still hunting for the killers of other victims. A champion runner, Bruce Lindsay Walker, had been missing since January. His chained and weighted body was found washed up on a beach. A 41-year-old woman had been stabbed 14 times while her 18-month-old baby son lay nearby. And a man was blasted to death with a shotgun when he opened his front door at Yarrambat, near Whittlesea, a town north-east of Melbourne.

There was another somber event not long after, but this time it had nothing to do with crime. Australia's longest serving Prime Minister, Sir Robert Gordon Menzies, died from a heart attack while reading in his study at his home in the Melbourne suburb of Malvern on May 15, 1978. He had led the country from 1939 to 1941 and again from 1949 to 1966. A state funeral was held at Scots Church on Collins Street in central Melbourne.

The Herald's chief political correspondent Peter Bowers came down to join me in Melbourne, and we covered the funeral together. Under a joint byline in the next day's paper, we wrote:

> Melbourne, under a leaden sky, gave Sir Robert Menzies the simple funeral he wanted, but it was simplicity touched with greatness and solemn ceremony. Inside Scots Church the nation's leaders sat shoulder to shoulder and with world statesmen, politicians, and royalty – Prince Charles, representing the Queen.

Menzies was known for many things, and one of them was his devotion to the Queen. When she came to Australia in

1963 and visited Parliament House in Canberra, he famously looked at her as he ended his welcoming speech and expressed his admiration for her by sharing lines from English poet Thomas Ford's poem, *There Is a Lady Sweet and Kind*:

> I did but see her passing by,
>
> And yet I love her till I die.

Looking back, it was hardly a simple funeral. More than 700 Australian and foreign dignitaries attended the event, protected by a massive security operation comprising 3,000 police, including an anti-terrorist unit. When the body was moved from the church to Springvale Crematorium 15 km away, police estimated that between 70,000 and 100,000 people lined the route to pay their respects.

At the crematorium, the funeral procession was met by a lone piper and the melancholy skirl of the Scottish lament, *Flowers of the Forest*. The brief service, attended only by members of Menzies family, ended with a 19-gun salute.

Murder and funeral aside, union disputes were a mainstay of the Melbourne Bureau news coverage. They were frequent and often angry, although they weren't always in Melbourne. There was a good reason for these stories landing on my plate. Someone living in Melbourne was a central figure in nearly every major industrial dispute that broke out.

He was Robert James Lee Hawke, or Bob Hawke, who at the time was President of the Australian Council of Trade Unions (ACTU), and, in the not-too-distant future, destined to enter politics and eventually become one of Australia's most loved prime ministers.

Hawke was a larrikin, with a reputation for flirting with the ladies … and drinking. But he was also a master negotiator, who would arrive in the middle of a dispute and somehow work out a deal acceptable to both sides. Best of all, from our point of view, he was extremely media-friendly. I would phone him at home in the early evening to check if there were any developments in a story I was writing to ensure when I filed it the piece was bang up to date.

'I'm in the middle of dinner,' he would say. 'Call me back in 30 minutes.' When I did, the phone would be picked up on the first ring, and he would happily update me on affairs and answer any question I had.

My first experience of his skill was in SA, and the dispute involved 12 maritime, transport and rural unions. At issue was the export of live sheep from Australia to the Middle East, where the animals had to be slaughtered under halal (it means *permissible* in Arabic) rituals based on Islamic law. The animal must be alive and healthy, and a Muslim must perform the slaughter. The trade was worth more than $300 million annually to Australia's economy.

The problem was that various maritime and transport unions had decided the trade was inhumane. They imposed bans and went on strike. It had been going on for three weeks and had escalated into two national strikes involving meatworkers and waterside workers, who were refusing to load the sheep on ships waiting at ports in SA and WA.

This, naturally, enraged the farmers and their unions, the Australian Wool Growers and Graziers' Council, and the Australian Wool and Meat Producers' Federation.

They decided to take matters into their own hands and load the sheep themselves. About 600 farmers, including many from NSW, took part in a secret pre-dawn operation in which they managed to truck 20,000 sheep to the little port of Wallaroo, on the Spencer Gulf, 100 km north of Adelaide. There, a ship, the *Aries Chief*, was waiting, having been diverted from Adelaide.

But meatworkers had heard what was happening and were heading for Wallaroo, where a massive confrontation seemed likely.

Enter Bob Hawke, arriving in Adelaide with me close on his tail. He said he was flying to the SA capital to try 'to prevent confrontation, violence and bloodshed'. After getting leaders of the warring parties together in three-and-a-half hours of negotiation, he emerged to announce the dispute had been settled. Hawke described it as one of the worst that had ever threatened Australia and said the bans on export of live sheep would be lifted the following morning.

That first year in Melbourne there seemed to be an endless series of disputes. Airline ground staff, members of the Transport Workers' Union (TWU), went on strike over a pay increase.

The Arbitration Commission had awarded them rises of between $11 and $24 but the airlines, international flag-carrier Qantas and domestic operators Trans Australia Airlines (TAA) and Ansett, appealed against the award, which was then reduced by $7.10 and $14 in the two groups. The unions went on strike, and air services were drastically reduced. Enter Bob Hawke once again. After seven hours of private talks initiated by the ACTU leader, a compromise was worked out.

Airlines were hit again as the peak Christmas holiday season approached. Tanker drivers, also members of the TWU, went on strike, once again over a pay rise. Strikes and bans by 4,000 TWU members employed at airports around the country cut air services by 70%.

A long conference between representatives of airlines, the TWU, and Hawke once again produced a compromise. There was more industrial turbulence involving transport. Some 33,000 public transport workers went on strike stopping trains, buses, and trams in Victoria, SA, and Tasmania. Then a row erupted between Telecom Australia and the Australian Telecommunications Employees' Union (ATEU) over claims for a 20% pay rise. Workers refused to carry out maintenance, and telecommunications across the country were disrupted.

In the middle of all this industrial mayhem, there was tragedy. Melbourne has two airports. Tullamarine is the major facility, handling international and domestic jet services.

A few kilometers away, Essendon Airport serves business jet and light aircraft operations. On July 10, 1978, a light aircraft lost power shortly after taking off from

Essendon. It plunged to the ground, leapfrogged an airport perimeter fence, crossed the busy Tullamarine Freeway, and smashed through three suburban houses. The fuel tanks erupted on impact, spraying fuel over one of the homes.

The flash fire that ensued resulted in the deaths of six members of one family. They were Mrs Pauline Gulle, 30, her mother, Mrs Margaret Thomas, 60, and Mrs Gulle's four children, Michael, 12, Sharon, 10, Robert, six, and Graham, one month.

Superintendent John Moore of the Eastern Hill fire station told me: 'They had no chance. It was a flash fire. The bodies of the six were unrecognizable.' What made this even more tragic was that Mr Sam Gulle was away from the house at the time, preparing their new property near Ballarat, west of Melbourne, for the arrival of his family in about a fortnight.

It was part and parcel of a reporter's lot. Each day, something different. Whether it was industrial disputation, crime, or human tragedy, you had to be ready for anything. And it wasn't all serious.

In February 1979, a story appeared under my name with the headline 'Och! But d'ye ken it's not cricket?' It was about the famous Melbourne Cricket Ground, scene of Test match cricket and Australian Rules football matches, undergoing a transformation.

'In their place will be the battlements of a Scottish castle and the stirring sounds of the pipes and drums,' I wrote. 'The metamorphosis is in aid of a new venture the city's fathers hope will help put Melbourne on the map, a full-scale military tattoo similar to the Edinburgh Tattoo.' It was being staged over ten nights in March and April and would feature 15 military bands, including the famous Gordon Highlanders. I'm not sure, but the heading may have been a sub-editor's nod to my Scottish heritage.

Away from the news, we were also enjoying pleasant weekend breaks. Sometimes by ourselves, sometimes with some of the other bureau chiefs and their families. A favorite jaunt was to the wine regions in northern Victoria, such as Rutherglen, or to Mount Buller, in Victoria's High Country. It was also a ski center, but we weren't into that particular pastime. In summer it was attractive country to drive through, with the odd deer or brumbies, wild horses, to be seen.

And there were birthdays to celebrate. Both mine and Tracey's were in July, and one year, on my birthday, Roz suddenly said she felt like some beer and sent me out to the pub to get some. When I got back, about 20 people there screamed 'Surprise!' at me. The WA Bureau Chief David Hummerstone and his wife Janet had made a fantastic birthday cake in the shape of a typewriter. The paper in the typewriter had typed on it: 'From Tom Ballantyne in Melbourne' and the brand name on the typewriter said 'MacRemington'.

A few days later there was Tracey's sixth birthday, and a dozen kids roaring around the house. In a letter shortly afterwards to my parents in Edinburgh, I wrote:

> She did, of course, get all the things she wanted. A new pram for her dolls, a train set and a

skateboard. She loves the skateboard and now alternates between the skates (roller) she got for Xmas and the skateboard.

While there continued to be a variety of industrial disputes – clearly the unions wanted to maintain their reputation for extreme strike action – one issue dominated the first half of 1980: the upcoming Summer Olympics in Moscow, the first to be staged in an Eastern Bloc country. Eighty nations were represented at the games, the smallest number since 1956. Sixty-six countries boycotted the games entirely because of the Soviet Union's war in Afghanistan.

US President Jimmy Carter had issued an ultimatum in January, stating the US would boycott the Olympics if Soviet troops did not withdraw from Afghanistan within one month.

In Australia, debate continued on whether it should send a team or not. Prime Minister Malcolm Fraser wanted Australia to join the boycott. The Australian Olympic Federation was dithering. It was based in Melbourne, and sportswriter Jim Webster came down from Sydney to work on the stories with me. There were endless federation meetings and continual postponements of a decision.

In late June the federation executive rejected a final call by Fraser not to send a team. Australian athletes would go to Moscow. Fraser expressed dismay and regret, saying the decision represented 'a failure of executive leadership and a denial of national responsibility'.

While, in the end, some individual athletes did refuse to go, overall Australia had a poor games. It won only nine medals, two gold, two silver and five bronze, placing it 15th on the medals tally. Unsurprisingly, Communist bloc nations dominated. The top four countries were the Soviet Union, with 195 medals, East Germany with 126, Bulgaria with 41, and Cuba with 20.

Back in Melbourne, there was also the small matter of the painters and dockers, the Federated Ship Painters and Dockers Union – a union even Bob Hawke couldn't keep under control.

Its activities had nothing to do with industrial disputation. It was notorious for involvement in criminal activity. In September 1980, a joint Federal and Victorian State Government Royal Commission was set up to investigate these activities. Headed by Frank Costigan QC, it looked at numerous crimes, including a string of murders, assaults, tax-fraud networks, drug-trafficking syndicates, and intimidation.

For journalists, approaching the painters and dockers for comments on developments or allegations was fraught with danger. On several occasions I was told to 'F#@$! off or I'll kick your F#@$!ing head in'.

Apart from the commission sessions, there was plenty to write about. The secretary of the Victorian branch of the union, Jack 'Putty Nose' Nicholls was found dead in his car while en route to give evidence at the commission. Although ruled as a suicide, no-one bought that conclusion.

He himself had become the union's secretary after his predecessor, Pat Shannon, was murdered by Bill 'The Texan' Longley.

The Costigan Commission didn't conclude until 1984. It found that since 1971, the union had 'a positive policy of recruiting hardened criminals', who were essentially outsourced 'to any dishonest person requiring criminals to carry out his project'. The commission noted 15 murders in which painters and dockers members were either involved or in which the murder was related to union activities.

Costigan observed that:

> The Union has attracted to its ranks large numbers of men who have been convicted of, and who continue to commit, serious crimes', and that 'violence is the means by which they control the members of their group. They do not hesitate to kill.

Included in the crimes of union members were: 'taxation fraud, social security fraud, ghosting, compensation fraud, theft on a grand scale, extortion, the handling of massive importations of drugs, the shipments of armaments, all manner of violence and murder'.

Incredibly, the outcome didn't lead to deregistration of the union, although it did lead to the establishment of a National Crime Authority to investigate tax fraud and organized crime. The painters and dockers was eventually deregistered in 1993, not for any criminal activity but because it had fewer than 1,000 members.

In late 1980 I was approaching two years as Melbourne Bureau Chief. I was getting restless. No specific time limit had been set for my Victorian sojourn, but I wrote a personal memo to the News Editor, Alan Dobbyn, essentially saying that while any future position I might be appointed to at the SMH was obviously a decision for the editor, I wanted to give them an idea of my own ambitions.

With my background in bureau work, not only in Melbourne but with AANS in Salisbury, I was keen to do more, specifically in Canberra and, ultimately, somewhere like Washington. It may have been a little forward, but I didn't want to sit back and await decisions on my future without them knowing what my own feelings were. Of course, slots don't come up very often for plum bureau postings, particularly overseas, so I was quite prepared to be patient until something came along.

When I did return to Sydney it wasn't to anything special, just a few months in State Parliament covering politics and parliamentary sessions, as well as an NSW State election in 1981. Then months back at head office in the features department, writing about anything and everything. I can't say these were exciting times, but it all added up to more experience and a strengthening of my reputation as a good all-round journalist.

In early 1983 I was back in Melbourne again. Australia is the Lucky Country, the Sunburnt Country. It is also a land of extremes: droughts that last for years, floods that inundate towns, and bushfires.

In February that year, fires were raging across Victoria and SA. It was evident a serious catastrophe was underway. I was sent to coordinate our coverage. The peak of the fires came on February 16, ironically, Ash Wednesday. In just 12 hours, more than 180 fires, fanned by hot winds of up to 110 km/h, caused widespread destruction across both states. By day's end 75 people had died, 47 in Victoria and 28 in SA. Most of the fatalities were the result of firestorm conditions caused by sudden and violent wind changes. More than 2,000 homes were destroyed.

On the front page of the SMH, the headline declared 'There is nothing left...' with my byline on the story.

This was embarrassing. I was there as a coordinator. Our Melbourne reporters were the ones who had been out on the fire front, gathering news and reporting back to me. I sat safely in our bureau gathering their information, as well as additional material from reporters of the other interstate newspaper bureaus around me and various press releases issued by the authorities, the police, fire and emergency services.

Then, as deadline approached, my task was to pull it all together into a single lead story and two or three shorter break-out stories. The names of the journalists who had really done the hard work should have been included in the story.

I apologized to them and complained to head office. After all, I had been the victim of a similar thing in the past. A few years earlier I had made a major contribution to a story involving a Liberal pre-selection battle leading up to a federal election. When the story appeared, someone else's name was on it. Afterwards, the then-acting news editor Alan Peterson sent me an internal memo:

> Many thanks for the continued effort that produced the Liberal Party pre-selection story this morning. If in the long run we took advantage of the very long experience and special knowledge in this field of another reporter, we did so to strengthen a story which was already strong and exclusive. The credit for unearthing this story and getting it over the line for the first edition was yours.

It was scant reward. Bylines aren't simply an ego thing. They are vital cogs in a journalist's armory. The more your name appears in the newspaper, the more people recognize you. When you venture out on assignments, whether someone recognizes your name from the *Sydney Morning Herald* or not can make the difference between them talking or not talking.

My career was soon to take another turn, but before it did, I was back in the world of the military. This time, it wasn't in Australia or Africa. I embarked on a tour of North Atlantic Treaty Organization (NATO) bases around Europe. First to NATO headquarters in Brussels, where I quickly discovered that here it wasn't NATO, but OTAN – not simply a reversal of the term NATO, but the French version, the Organisation du Traité de l'Atlantique Nord.

The second discovery was more startling. These were Cold War years, and senior NATO officials, both military and civilian, told me if Warsaw Pact tanks were to roll across the border into Western Europe, it was almost certain that NATO forces would have to resort quickly to the use of nuclear weapons to prevent being overrun.

The reason: NATO had allowed its conventional forces to run down so much that the cost of catching up was now prohibitively high, and the armed forces of some NATO nations were simply not up to scratch. In other words, the West was outnumbered and totally outgunned. Thankfully, history tells us it didn't happen.

My next stop was Norway and its icy north, where 7,000 of its troops guarded a 196-km frontier with the Soviet Union – across the border, 27,000 Russian combat troops. I was told that what was called the Nordic Balance was backed up by Nordic cool and Norway had very diplomatically agreed with a Soviet request that no-one shoot photographs across the border.

'There is no tension', a senior Norwegian Defense Department official told me.

From there, it was on to Germany, first to a US Army base at Wurtzburg in northern Bavaria, close to the East German border.

There, I asked a lieutenant colonel I was interviewing about the red button on his desk. His response was to press it. Loud sirens blared across the camp and men came running from everywhere, some having clearly been in the middle of having a shower, before jumping into armored cars and racing out the gate. They would be directed to any hotspot or 'event' along the border fence. East German border guards often fired their Kalashnikovs into the air just to provoke a reaction.

Next stop was a flight to Berlin, behind the Iron Curtain, the city divided by that wall, where I interviewed a 23-year-old called Ralf Molder. He was a former lieutenant in the East German Border Guard who, one night, had hit his comrade over the head with his Makarov pistol and scaled the wall, complete with Makarov and Kalashnikov, to escape to West Berlin. He was now working as a handyman in the most unlikely of places, at a museum at Checkpoint Charlie, just a few meters from the East.

And East was where I went next. Under the postwar agreement that divided Berlin into different sectors – American, British, French, and Soviet – some foreigners were allowed to enter East Berlin from West Berlin, and America regularly sent diplomats and officials into the Soviet sector through Checkpoint Charlie. Two diplomats from the US Embassy took me through. They were probably CIA, but I didn't ask.

The two Berlins were like chalk and cheese. West Berlin was typically Western – bright lights, lively nightlife, stores full of high fashion and consumer goods. East Berlin was a picture of darkness – gloomy, drab, with all the hallmarks of a communist state. Propaganda posters were everywhere, shop windows full of messages about the workers and their deeds. No-one smiled.

There was a final stop, to Italy and the headquarters of the NATO Mediterranean fleet in Naples. Then, it was back to Australia and soon, that new twist in my career.

11

Pens down!

Like any other industry, in journalism, you can have ambitions and hopes but they don't always materialize. The possibility of that overseas bureau assignment arose when our London correspondent was returning to Sydney. There was hope in my heart, but it didn't last for long. Someone else got the post. I was certainly disappointed, but it seemed the Editor-in-Chief, Chris Anderson, had something else in mind.

For some time, I had been doing stints as acting CoS on Sundays, normally, though not always, a quieter news day. Then, in October 1983, I was appointed Deputy CoS. The role was as the title suggested, acting as assistant to CoS Frykberg, by taking some of the load from his shoulders and helping brief reporters. The downside, of course, was that I had to push the typewriter aside, for the time being at least. No more chasing stories; I was deskbound.

Working for the Buddha-like Frykberg was a joy. Born in South Africa, he had moved to New Zealand as a child and later to Sydney to further his journalistic career. He had been in London for the SMH and had covered politics in Canberra. He was the ultimate professional, someone you could learn much from. To the reporting staff, he was 'Frykers', and everyone loved him.

For me, 1984 turned out to be a pivotal year, and one of rapid change. In March I was promoted to A2 grade, and by July, another upgrade took me to Sp. A grade, or Special A grade. In early November, my salary was increased to $35,000 a year, including an expense allowance of $1,000, with my name added to the higher salaries list.

On December 18, I received another memo from the editor-in-chief telling me my salary was once again being raised, to $38,000 a year from January 1, 1985. This was at a time when the average annual salary in Australia was $19,000.

Another significant, more personal event occurred. Like millions of immigrants who had gone before, on August 15, 1984, I officially became an Australian after taking the Oath of Allegiance at a ceremony in Parramatta's Town Hall. Complete with Certificate of Australian Citizenship, a sprig of wattle, and an Australia icon, a meat pie, I entered a new phase of my life.

I had known for a long time that I would never live in Scotland again, or anywhere in Britain. Australia was now my permanent home. Of course, it had problems like everywhere else, but as far as I was concerned, it was the best country in the world – a multicultural society where people of all races and religions mostly lived life in peace.

I quickly applied for and received an Australian passport. Being a dual citizen, with both an Australian and a British passport, was open to me, but I didn't see the point. When the British passport I held lapsed in November 1985, it wasn't renewed.

There was a reason for the promotions and pay rises that had come my way through the year. Frykberg had stepped down as CoS, and I naturally expected that, as his deputy, I would take his place, but it was not to be. Instead, another journalist, Paul Sheehan, was given the post.

He was one of those seen by senior management as destined for great things. A golden boy! I was disappointed, and frankly, furious, but I simply had to grit my teeth and accept the situation. Thankfully, it didn't last for long.

After a few short months Sheehan moved on, and I became CoS. The job came with a few perks. Apart from a higher salary, the company paid our full home telephone account, and at 7.30 each morning, one of the company's radio cars would be waiting outside our home to drive me into the office.

As soon as I got in, I would be on the radio to my secretary to find out what was happening, if any early stories were breaking and if any messages had to be passed on to me from various editors.

In the newsroom, the first few hours were hectic. Every day, there was a news conference at 10 am to discuss the day's stories, and I had to prepare a news list. All the specialist reporters covering various rounds had to be spoken to. What were they working on? Did they have any exclusive stories? What was happening in police rounds? What were the stories developing in NSW state politics and federal politics in Canberra? Were there any stories in this morning's paper that needed to be followed up? We had a diary of upcoming events, such as important court cases. What was in the diary for the day?

The 10 am news conference was held in the editor-in-chief's office. It was attended by all and sundry: the foreign editor, the features editor, the news editor, the sports editor, various other deputy editors and associate editors. And me, the center of attention. Everyone had a copy of the news list, and I would go through each story, one by one, explaining what it was about, who was writing it, and what I expected it to produce at the end of the day.

It was, essentially, a free-for-all. When I was finished, anyone could contribute suggestions for new stories, or for different angles on the ones we had. There would be discussion about which stories on the list had the potential to be the front-page lead story in the next day's paper. The editor-in-chief might comment that he had picked up an interesting snippet of information over dinner with some notable the previous night. I would nominate someone to investigate and follow it up. And there were, of course, some ridiculous suggestions that had absolutely no hope of bearing fruit. Nevertheless, I had to assign some poor reporter to the task.

Post-conference was just as hectic. Reporters had to be reassigned to cover new, suggested stories, or updated on fresh angles to investigate. The news is an ever-changing feast. As the day wore on, new stories would break, some big, some not so big. Would a single reporter do, or would two or more be required? Who was best suited for the job?

The final news conference of the day was at 4 pm. There was an updated news list. Some potential stories had fallen through. Others had become more interesting. A story that had been seen as a possible front-page lead had fallen flat. I had to explain to the editors, diplomatically, why their suggestions had failed to materialize into anything positive. All in all, you were walking a daily tightrope, under constant pressure trying to make possible the impossible.

Nor was being CoS all about producing news lists and assigning the right reporters to the right tasks. You had to be a 'mother', something of a psychologist. Reporters are people. They have worries at home and in the office. They get upset about being asked to do something they think might be a waste of their energy. And they get disappointed if you criticize what they have done, or if asked to rewrite a story because I thought it needed a different treatment, a different intro.

There were 300 journalists under my control, and each had a different personality. Of course, the sports journalists reported first to the sports editor, the business journalists to their editor, but ultimately the buck stopped with me, answerable only to the editor-in-chief. I had to have the ability to manage people, to talk people through issues they had.

The newsroom was full of characters. Malcolm Brown, undoubtedly our best general reporter, had the fastest shorthand of anyone I've ever known and could always be relied on to produce the goods. But he was moody. One time he got upset at something while out on an assignment, ripped the car radio from its bracket and threw it out the window. I was one of the few people who could calm him down when the sparks began to fly.

Another was David, or Davey, Robertson, the Motoring Editor, who was my closest friend at the Herald. He was another Scot, from the Kingdom of Fife on the opposite bank of the Firth of Forth from Edinburgh. Always grinning and full of life, he could be outrageous at times.

We had a young reporter called Carol Thatcher, the daughter of British Prime Minister Margaret Thatcher, who was starting her long journalistic career in Sydney at the Herald. One day the newsroom was startled when she let out a piercing scream. Davey had crept up behind her, thrown his arms around her and squeezed both of her breasts. Miss Thatcher was not amused, although most of the newsroom broke out into waves of laughter.

Of course, today that sort of thing would probably and rightly end up with a sexual assault charge in court. Back then it was a different age, and such things were mostly regarded as a bit of innocent fun. Tragically, David died in a jet-ski accident almost a decade later, in February 1994, while attending a barbecue beach party put on by a motoring company.

The tribute at his funeral says it all:

> The most compact stars shine brightest. So much was packed into David Robertson's diminutive frame that he seemed larger than life, certainly larger than his size. He would fairly bounce into the room, cheery 'hello' to greet everyone as if this were a special day and he had its measure. He treated every day as special, something to be lived completely in the present, for why worry about tomorrow? Life would look after itself – after all, hadn't it so far? He made the sun shine on himself through sheer force of will and then he had the grace to pretend that simple good fortune was behind it all. His span was so brief, but how brilliant!

They were fitting words, and it was also fitting that as his funeral ceremony came to an end, he was farewelled with the haunting sound of a bagpipe lament.

Aside from its seasoned reporters, each year the Herald took on half a dozen new cadet reporters. Many of them had completed the Bachelor of Arts (Communication – Journalism) course at Charles Sturt University in Bathurst, on the western side of the Blue Mountains. But all the newcomers had degrees of one sort or another, and some of the people who wanted to become journalists were surprising, for example, a young doctor, whose initial career choice would have been far more lucrative.

However, on the question of qualifications, I was at odds with the editor. Being old-school, I believed we should employ some applicants who didn't have degrees but who clearly had a passion for journalism. I often wonder how many young people who had not gone through university but who, like me, had a burning ambition to get into journalism, weren't given the chance. I only hope that some succeeded by getting a reporting job at a smaller weekly or regional newspaper. Of course, there was no winning my argument. The editor had the final word.

Steering those new cadets through their first steps was part of the CoS's job. There were friendly, informal chats with each of them to get an idea of their personalities. What were their ambitions? Were they interested in politics, sport, the environment, or something else? Down the track, knowing those things would help in guiding their path. Of course, being bright young things, they were all ambitious and keen to move quickly.

I, on the other hand, being old-school, believed they should first get a good, all-round grounding and learn their trade from the ground up. This meant cycling them through different areas of news coverage: time on police rounds, time covering courts, then at State Parliament, and on general reporting duties, even a period on sports.

It was another area in which I clashed with the editor. By this time, it was Eric Beecher, at 33 the *Sydney Morning*

Herald's youngest-ever chief. Chris Anderson had moved up into Fairfax Group management. Like all editors, Beecher had his favorites among the cadets, with one or two earmarked to rise quickly through the ranks. He didn't want them to waste time on police rounds or the like. Again, it was an argument I couldn't win, but I still believe that getting that good, all-round grounding is the making of the best professional journalist.

Years later, some of those cadets, now fully fledged and experienced journalists, told me I was the best chief of staff they had ever worked for. I told them I had been fortunate, having overseen the newsroom during a golden period at the Herald. My job was made easy because of the standard of reporting and the rounds people I had at the time. People like Keith Martin, industrial correspondent; Joseph Glascott, covering the environment; Shaun McIlraith, medical correspondent; Alan Gill, the church reporter; and of course, Peter Bowers, Mike Steketee, and columnist Paul Kelly in Canberra. They all churned out exclusive after exclusive, keeping us miles ahead of rival newspapers such as News Corps' *The Australian*. All in all, it made me look very good at those daily news conferences.

It should also be said that many of these cadets went on to have highly rewarding careers in journalism. Brad Norington left the Herald and joined *The Australian*, where he achieved something that I didn't, becoming its Washington Correspondent during the presidency of Barack Obama. Returning to Australia, he became an associate editor, writing about national affairs and NSW politics. He married Jennifer Cooke, another cadet who had spent a period with me in the Melbourne Bureau and was the best court reporter I ever knew.

Peter Hartcher became the SMH Political and International Editor. Richard Glover ended up at the Australian Broadcasting Corporation (ABC) with his own radio show, *Thank God It's Friday*. Paola Totaro, an Italian-Australian journalist, was Europe correspondent for the Herald and *The Age*, Melbourne, and editor of the Saturday *Sydney Morning Herald*. Based in London, she was at one stage President of the Foreign Press Association and specializes in writing about European affairs, politics, social policy, and the arts. Of course, there were many more, and I only hope that as chief of staff I played a small role in guiding them through those early years in journalism.

I spent three years as chief of staff and could have stayed a lot longer, but the constant daily pressure and long hours certainly took their toll. The time had come to step down and do something else.

12

Back in front of a typewriter

One of the bonuses of being chief of staff is that it is a little like being the President of the US. When you do step down, you keep all the perks – apart from the car picking you up at home every day – and you pretty much get to pick what you want to do next.

There were two choices: move up another rung of the ladder and become a deputy editor or associate editor or the like, or go back to writing. For me, it was a no-brainer. There was no way I wanted to continue sitting behind a desk. For me, it was a return to writing.

Again, my timing was perfect. As it happened, our Travel and Aviation Editor Ben Sandilands was resigning to join the staff of *The Bulletin*, a weekly magazine first published in 1880. It focused on politics and business, with some literary content, and was Australia's longest-running magazine publication until its final issue in January 2008. For me, Ben's departure was a godsend. That, I immediately thought, is just the job for me. My typewriting fingers were itching to get going again.

We were sorry to see Ben go. He was a more-than-able reporter and certainly dedicated. When I was CoS, I sent him out one day to do a feature on what had become a popular pastime, hang-gliding. He had to go to the sand dunes at Cronulla, a southern Sydney suburb, and take lessons in the sport. Next thing we knew he was in hospital, having launched himself from a high dune and promptly crashed nose-first to the ground. I can't remember what his exact injuries were, but he certainly had broken bones and, I think, some sort of minor spinal damage. Yet he still filed the story ... from his hospital bed.

My first opportunity to travel had come before I left the CoS desk. Ken Morton, the Sydney-based regional public relations director for British Airways (BA), aware I was soon to become travel and aviation editor, invited me to fly to London to interview the airline's chairman. He was Lord King, or more formally Lord King of Wartnaby. Best of all, Ken, who was to become a lifetime, valued friend, had arranged for me to fly first class. It was the first time I had experienced being up front in an aircraft, and it was surreal to reflect how a lad from a working-class Edinburgh background could be in such illustrious company, being treated like a VIP.

As for Lord King, talk about self-aggrandizement! The walls of his office in central London were almost completely covered with photographs – Lord King with US President Jimmy Carter, with President Ronald Reagan, with Prince

Charles, with, it seemed, the entire contents of *Who's Who*. But he was a good interviewee. Lord King had been put into a government-owned BA by Prime Minister Margaret Thatcher to prepare it for privatization.

The carrier had been suffering staggering annual losses of around $760 million and was in a woeful state. King wasted no time. The airline's staff of 58,200 was slashed by more than 21,500, bringing the number down to 36,700. In three years, he had closed 37 of its international and 25 domestic routes, shut down 25 of its stations, and three maintenance bases around the world. Some 82 aircraft were withdrawn from service, and 60 of them were sold for $135 million. He made it clear to me that government-run businesses were not his cup of tea.

'Governments are not designed to be profit-making enterprises,' he said.

King was often described as a surgeon for the slashing that was occurring under his guidance.

'I don't know that I was the surgeon. All I did was put a board of nationally minded people together and introduce good housekeeping,' he explained. In his short time at BA, he turned those losses into huge profits.

Back in Sydney, I had left behind a newsroom that was open-plan. From the CoS desk you could see everything: all the reporters, the subs desk, the sports department, and other areas. When I finally left the position, I moved into my own private office, though there were many times it would be unoccupied.

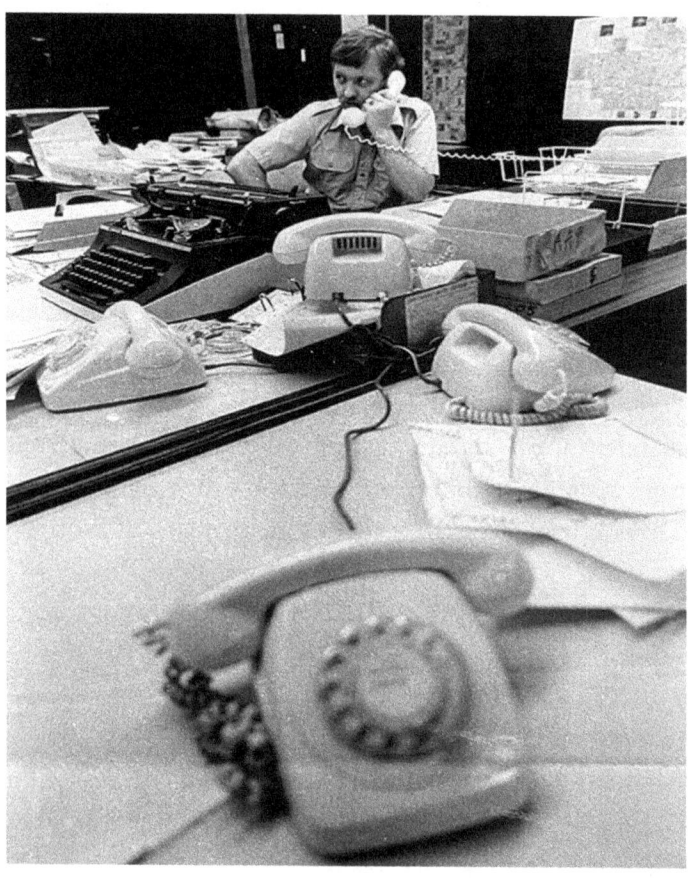

Early days at the Sydney Morning Herald. The beginning of a great 18-year career with Australia's leading daily newspaper, which ultimately led to my appointment as chief of staff and then travel and aviation editor.

Having two titles, travel editor and aviation editor, was interesting. There was obvious crossover between them, but they were also different in many ways. Travel involved news coverage; stories about cheap airfares; the best hotel deals; a surge in inbound tourists from Japan, China or elsewhere; and Australian government campaigns to attract increasing numbers of foreign tourists, always a boost to the economy.

But much of it involved feature-writing for our weekly travel supplements, traveling within Australia and overseas, and it wasn't always as attractive as many in the office thought.

For example, a hotel chain would invite you to the site of a new hotel or resort they were building. That was exactly what it was – a building site. They would drag you around, enthusiastically proclaiming this is where reception will be, this is where the restaurants will be, this is where the pool will be, this is where the VIP rooms will be. In the end, without seeing the finished product, there wasn't much you could write about.

Many of the trips were organized by tourism authorities as group tours. Six to ten travel writers from around the country would be invited. The problem with that was they were all from different sections of the media, from newspapers and magazines to trade publications and television.

We all had different agendas, not to mention the agenda of the tourism body itself. The result was that half your time was spent seeing things and hearing things you were never going to write about. On one group trip to Norfolk Island, we were all bundled into a bus to take us to visit virtually every bed-and-breakfast and hotel establishment on the island.

Now Norfolk Island is a very interesting place. Administered by Australia, it is a former penal colony, where the worst convicts were sent from Sydney. Many of its residents are direct descendants of the *Bounty* mutineers, some of whom had been moved there from their bolt hole on Pitcairn Island in the 1850s. Another journalist and I abandoned the bus after a short time, probably to the annoyance of the organizers, to seek out our own stories. We weren't going to be reporting on the details of every accommodation option on Norfolk Island.

My preference was always to travel alone. I didn't want to be led by the nose. When the British Tourist Authority office in Sydney invited me to tour the United Kingdom, I made it very clear to them: I don't want you to set some sort of itinerary. Just book me into a few key hotels around the country and have a rental car waiting for me at Heathrow. I'll take it from there and root out my own stories. It was the same on trips to the US, Canada, and elsewhere.

With an upcoming special supplement on travel to the US, I would be away for two weeks and opted to have company. We decided Tracey, now 12, would skip school and accompany me. Our view was that travel is a learning experience, teaching you about new cultures, how people live in other countries, seeing some of the wonders of the world. We talked to the principal of her school, and she agreed.

We flew to Los Angeles. With daughter in hand, there were, of course, obligatory visits to Disneyland and Universal Studios. After that, I was looking for something different, and I found it. The Forest Lawn Memorial Park at Glendale, California, just 10 minutes from downtown Los Angeles. A cemetery.

My fascination with graveyards may have originated with that visit to Beethoven's grave in Vienna many years before, but wandering between the tombstones of the rich and not-so-rich, the famous and not-so-famous, was somehow fulfilling, evoking thoughts of the past. And Forest Lawn wasn't just a cemetery. This was Hollywood, and here were the last resting places of great movie stars and notables such as Mary Pickford, WC Fields, Humphrey Bogart, Spencer Tracy, Clark Gable, Walt Disney, and Australian-born Errol Flynn.

Another Herald travel assignment. Tales from the USA. Here, the last resting place of Australian-born film star Errol Flynn in the Forest Lawn Memorial Park at Glendale, California, just 10 minutes from downtown Los Angeles. A cemetery with a touch of Hollywood.

There was more. In true Hollywood style, a gigantic theater, every hour, screened a film depicting the Crucifixion, accompanied by the sound of thunder and lightning. The entire show revolved around a religious painting by Polish master Jan Styka called *The Crucifixion*, a work of art 60 m long and 14 m high. Forest Lawn is a beautiful place. It may be a cemetery, but it has more than 10,000 trees, 100,000 shrubs, 125 acres of lawn, and hundreds of original works of art in bronze, marble, and stained glass.

Open every day of the year, the park attracts more than one million visitors annually, although they can't ramble around all the last resting places of the stars. Many of them are in private areas, accessible only to relatives with a key. That made a travel feature with the headline: 'The greatest cemetery show on earth'.

We weren't finished with graves. Moving on to Montana, we visited the site of the Battle of the Little Big Horn, where Lieutenant Colonel George Armstrong Custer and 298 of his men from the 7th Cavalry regiment met their end at the hands of a combined force of Lakota Sioux, Northern Cheyenne, and Arapaho Indian tribes.

If there is one thing America does well, it is preserving places of historical interest. There is, naturally, an information center at the battle site. Dotted around the slopes nearby are groups of tombstones, spread over several hectares. Only the graves of officers have names on them. All the others say something like, 'Soldier of the US 7th Cavalry died here. March 1876'.

When their comrades arrived at the scene of the massacre, they simply buried each man where he fell. If I thought I felt the presence of Custer here, I would have been wrong. Below the gravestone that marks where he died, there is nothing. His body was moved years ago to rest in the grounds of the military academy at West Point.

There was more. Montana and Wyoming were cowboy country. Here you could find characters of the old West. A tombstone that declared 'Blind Bill, murdered March 1894' or another that said 'Bill Wheaton, he died with his boots on'. There was Jeremiah 'liver-eating' Johnston, a giant of a mountain man who apparently had eaten his last liver.

Then, at the Arlington National Cemetery in Virginia, overlooking the Potomac River, we visited another goldmine of the departed. Buried here is President John F Kennedy; his brother Robert; world heavyweight boxing champion Joe Louis; Audie Murphy, film star and America's most decorated World War II hero; US astronauts Virgil Grissom and Roger Chaffee; Daniel 'Chappie' James Jnr, the first Black four-star general, and explorer Richard Byrd. All of this made another great and offbeat travel piece that appeared under the banner 'Bones Away From Home'.

I don't want anyone to get the idea I'm fixated with cemeteries. For me it was just a matter of finding something different. To many people, travel is sitting on a beach in Bali or Fiji, or Spain or Italy. To me it's a never-ending adventure. So, beyond the cemetery visits, there were plenty of other delights to experience.

Being based in Sydney, the South Pacific and its numerous palm-fringed islands beckoned. There were trips to Fiji, Samoa, Tonga, the Cook Islands, Papua New Guinea, the Solomon Islands, French Polynesia, Vanuatu, New Caledonia, and Tahiti. For me, the jewel among them all was Bora Bora, a tiny island group which is part of the Society Islands of French Polynesia, with a total land area of just 30.55 square km (12 square miles).

The airport was on a long, narrow strip of land that protected the main island from Pacific waves, creating a stunning lagoon. You were taken to your hotel by boat, over water so crystal clear it was like floating on air. Exotic, tropical fish and colorful coral could be clearly seen.

One of the main pastimes for visitors? Swimming with sharks. I was taken out on the lagoon with a few other tourists. Supplied with snorkels, we had to jump into the water and wait. A burly islander, who cleverly stayed in the boat, threw food scraps into the lagoon, which immediately attracted a swarm of sharks, which launched a frenzied attack on the food.

I admit, they were reef sharks, not large white pointers or hammerheads. Medium-sized. Nevertheless, it seemed to me they had very sharp teeth. Some of them got quite close and, I thought, wouldn't have a clue whether they were eating the food scraps or someone's fingers. Anyhow,

I emerged with ten fingers intact and another experience to remember.

A different kind of experience occurred on South Korea's Jeju Island. Off the country's south coast, it's a favorite destination for Korean and Japanese honeymooners because the island is dotted with statues called Dol Hareubangs, carved from volcanic rock and up to three meters high. The statues' faces feature grinning expressions, bulging eyes without pupils, long, broad noses, and faint smiles, and their hands rest on their bellies, one slightly above the other. They are considered gods, offering both protection and fertility, which is why the honeymoon couples have their photo taken while touching the statues.

My offbeat experience didn't involve fertility. It was to do with food. I stopped at a waterfront restaurant to have a meal, which meant selecting live seafood from a tank. I chose an octopus and expected it to eventually arrive well-cooked. It didn't take long, and it quickly became evident why delivery had been so speedy.

I was the recipient of a Korean delicacy, live octopus. Well, it was a deceased creature, but it had been chopped up so quickly that the pieces still thought they were alive. Bits of octopus tentacle were moving across the plate, presumably trying to escape. When you put one in your mouth, they suckered themselves to your tongue and you had to use a chopstick to force them free.

There was no choice but to struggle on since the proud restaurant owner was standing by to ensure his foreign guest was happy. In the end, it wasn't fatal, and it added another unforgettable gourmet memory to the scrapbook of life.

Unusual tales were everywhere. On a visit to Canada, at the invitation of Canada's tourism authorities, I flew to the Yukon Territory and Dawson City, heart of the Klondike Gold Rush, the only place in Canada where there was a legal casino, and it bore the name Diamond Tooth Gertie's. There, I had a flutter on the roulette wheel and came up trumps, winning enough cash to buy a pendant for my wife, with a nugget of real Yukon gold. But the find of the trip was undoubtedly the Sourtoe cocktail.

The story concerned a mummified big toe. In the Prohibition days of the 1920s, brothers Otto and Louie Liken, gold miners and trappers, were allegedly running rum across the border to Alaska when, one day, Louie's foot crashed through the snow into water. His big toe was frozen, a condition that could lead to gangrene. With no doctor within miles, Otto chopped his brother's toe off with an ax. They pickled the toe in alcohol and kept it in a jar on a shelf in their cabin.

Enter Captain Dick Stevenson, who in the 1970s found the jar and the petrified toe in the now-deserted cabin. I met Captain Dick in the Sluice Box Lounge of the Eldorado Hotel in Dawson City, where he told me how the cocktail had come about.

A few nights after finding the toe and after drinking copious amounts of alcohol, he dreamed up the ground rules for drinking the sour toe cocktail These original rules were to fill a beer glass with champagne, drop the toe in and drink, tipping back the glass until the toe touched the lips.

'You can drink it fast, you can drink it slow – but the lips have gotta touch the toe,' he explained. Just the sort of thing an eccentric riverboat captain would think of.

The cocktail became a rite of passage, and still is today, for anyone drinking in Dawson City. Thousands of tourists have joined the Sourtoe Cocktail Club and have certificates to prove it.

I wasn't one of them, and at the time, the toe wasn't the original one. It lasted only seven years, until a miner named Garry Younger attempted to break the record for the number of cocktails drunk. On his 13th glass of Sourtoe champagne, his chair tipped over backward, and he swallowed the toe. Sadly, it was not recovered.

However, there was no problem getting a replacement. Over the years, there have been a number of amputated toes donated, one due to an inoperable corn, one from a victim of frostbite, and yet another, due to diabetes.

One toe was stolen and became one of the strangest cases pursued by the Royal Canadian Mounted Police. They finally tracked the thief down in Fort Worth, Texas, and threatened to charge him with transporting a stolen body part across an international border. They told him no charges would be laid if he returned it, which was duly done.

'Not only do the Mounties get their man, but also their toe,' Captain Dick told me.

This was a time of technological change at the SMH. The computer age had arrived, and typewriters were disappearing from reporters' desks. No more carbon copies. It was a shock for some, who found it hard to adjust. Not for me. It made life so much easier. Company laptops were provided when traveling. You could write your story and, with the push of a button, send it off to the subeditors. And I didn't often have to file stories from overseas.

On most trips I could wait until I was back in Sydney and write in the office.

When I did have to write on the move and get a piece back in time for the deadline, a cumbersome piece of equipment had to be carried. It connected your laptop to the phone in the hotel room, or to the phone socket, which was another problem. Every country, particularly in Europe, has a different phone socket. I had to go out, find a store, and buy the required cable. They were taken back to Sydney and handed to the computer people, who could then dish out the suitable cable for whatever country a reporter was visiting.

One of the benefits of being travel editor was that now and again we could merge my trips with a family holiday. Such was the case on one tour of Britain, when Roz and Tracey came with me. We headed to Scotland to visit my parents, then collected a hire car and all of us drove to the

Isle of Skye. There, Mum, Dad and Tracey stayed in a bed-and-breakfast establishment, while Roz and I settled down in the comfort of Kinloch Lodge, accommodation organized by the British Tourist Authority.

This was no ordinary hotel, but the family home of Lord Godfrey and Lady Claire Macdonald. He had inherited the High Chieftainship of the Clan Macdonald, the largest of Scotland's Highland clans, in the 1970s. Kinloch Lodge wasn't only their home; they ran it as a remarkable hotel. Lady Macdonald was an award-winning cookery writer, which meant the fare was as good as it gets. When we dined in the evening, our dishes were served by Lord Macdonald himself, the highest-class waiter I have ever had. And again, I experienced that surreal feeling of wondering how someone with my background could be here.

I wrote glowingly of this very different travel experience, starting my feature:

> The first thing that strikes you about Kinloch Lodge is the silence. The second is the decidedly charming nature of its proprietors. The third is definitely the food. The silence is the silence of the Isle of Skye, of lone seagulls gliding in an icy breeze, bracken-coloured water lapping on a deserted beach and the strange desolation of the heather-covered moorland. Surrounded by all of that is Kinloch Lodge, white-painted and

lonely, standing at the head of Loch Na Dal, its windows facing southwards to the dramatic mountains of Knoydart on the Scottish mainland and west to the mysterious, mist-covered Cuillin range of Skye.

One of the delights of traveling in Britain is the endless number of quaint, country inns, particularly in Scotland. There you meet locals and sit by warm peat fires sipping Scotch and listening to local yarns.

One such place was Creggans Inn, on the banks of Loch Fynn. It was owned by Sir Fitzroy MacLean, war hero, traveler, diplomat, former member of parliament, author, and founder member of the elite SAS, who was said to have been the inspiration for Ian Fleming's iconic secret agent, James Bond, 007.

Creggans had its own whisky, Old MacPhunn, whose ingredients were reputed to include a dash of mother's milk. The legend came about because centuries ago a local laird, MacPhunn of Drip, had taken to sheep-stealing and was caught and hanged at Inverary, on the opposite side of Loch Fyne from Creggans. His widow collected the corpse and was rowing back across the loch. Pregnant at the time, she mixed some of her own milk with whisky and forced it between her dead husband's lips, at which point he sat up, fully revived.

Cartoonists had a ball with my Scottish roots. Just to set the record straight, I've never had Scotch for breakfast.

By law, he couldn't be hanged twice and so lived happily for many years and now lies buried in Strachur churchyard, near the inn. Fact or fiction? Who cares? It is a great yarn.

On another family trip to Europe, I was to fly from London to Moscow to visit Russia's national airline Aeroflot. While I was away, Roz and Tracey decided to fly down to Spain and visit Barcelona. On the morning they were leaving, we hopped into our rental car, and I drove them to Heathrow to catch their flight. Try as we might, we couldn't find it on the departure board. When I finally resorted to asking someone, we were told, 'That flight doesn't leave from here, it leaves from Gatwick' – London's second airport, kilometers away on the other side of the city.

We bundled back into the car, and I drove like a mad thing, getting them there in time for them to board the plane just before the doors were closed. Another lesson learned, especially for a travel and aviation writer. When a city has more than one airport, always check which one your plane is at.

As for Moscow, it was the coldest place I've ever been, so cold I couldn't take my hands from my pockets to snap photographs. But I still have a memento. These were the days when most airlines gave their business-class passengers a small gift. In the Russian airlines case, for male passengers, it was a bottle of cologne somewhat ironically called 'Aeroflot Deluxe'. I'm pretty sure it was watered-down jet fuel.

Years later I still have it. It's still full, and it still smells like watered-down jet fuel. This was in stark contrast to the gift another airline, the Netherland's Royal Dutch Airlines (KLM), gave passengers. It was a small porcelain model of

Dutch buildings, full of gin. I still have a few of these but, I can assure you, they are now all empty.

Oh, and then there was the time I met Santa Claus. On a trip to Finland, en route to Finnish Lapland, I stopped at Rovaniemi, considered by Finns to be the official hometown of Santa Claus.

Santa lives in Santa Claus Village inside the Arctic Circle, and the great man was happy to greet me with his usual beaming smile. Many of the letters sent to Santa by children ended up here, and he explained to me there were so many of them he now used a computer to write his replies.

There were many other experiences over the years I was travel editor, from a guided tour of the Pentagon in Washington and yachting in the Greek Islands, to visiting nearly every country in Asia.

During this time, I was also the travel correspondent for ABC radio's weekend show, hosted by John Hall. I would go into the studio and talk about travel, or if I was away, phone in from wherever I was and chat about the destination. I had my first book published by ABC Books. It was titled *Breakfast in Bali, Supper at the Savoy, a guide to trouble-free travel* and featured illustrations by SMH cartoonist Alan Moir.

While I wrote about the many travel experiences I had, there were numerous tips for travelers, including how to cope with the hassles of getting through the airport, how to deal with customs, overcoming language difficulties, eating abroad, lost baggage and much more.

Tourists often get caught up in the main events, or main attractions, and lose out. When it comes to eating in Tokyo, Japan, for example, steer clear of the famous Ginza strip. I ate in a hotel restaurant in the Ginza. The main course cost $200 and a three-course meal was more than $400. Thankfully, I wasn't paying; the bill was being taken care of by our airline host.

Just a couple of minutes' walk from the Ginza, in the alleys that run parallel, are dozens of restaurants where you get great food for next to nothing.

The Weekend Show team at ABC Radio 702, where I was also travel editor. I'm second from left and the show host, John Hall, is second from the right.

Like many travelers, lost baggage was something I had experienced. On the way back from a trip to Seattle visiting

American aircraft manufacturer Boeing, a photographer and I transited through San Francisco.

When we arrived back in Sydney, my suitcase failed to appear. In the end, Qantas paid me compensation for the lost goods. Two years later, a letter arrived from the San Francisco Police Department, advising me they had my suitcase. Apparently, they had busted a ring of thieves and discovered a warehouse full of bags, one of which was mine. It was sent to me, but when I opened it, not a single item was mine. Clearly, the thieves had ransacked the bags looking for valuables and randomly thrown things back in.

It had been quite a ride but my time as travel editor was coming to an end. I was aware a computer and technology editor wanted my job. He sweet-talked the editor into splitting off the travel portion of my position and appointing him in my place with the promise he could bring in lots of advertising dollars. In the end, I didn't argue.

He left the Herald a couple of years later after an episode of ABC television's *Media Watch* identified allegedly plagiarized material under his byline, insertions which, according to him, had been made by a junior colleague while he was on leave.

I knew differently. Sometime before, the press officer for Hong Kong's Cathay Pacific Airways in Sydney had shown me two travel features, pinned to a wall in her office. The first was from the *New York Times* by the original author. The second was from an edition of the Herald a few weeks later. They were identical apart from the fact the Herald feature was bylined with my colleague's name.

In the meantime, I was still aviation editor, I still had my private office, and Australia's aviation landscape was undergoing dramatic change, which would keep me more than busy over the coming years.

The things you had to do as Herald travel and aviation editor. A hostie at last! After a grueling eight-week training course with the Flying Kangaroo leading to working on a London-bound flight and a report on what it's really like to be airline cabin crew.

13

Frenzy in the air

As travel editor, I had also covered aviation. In between jaunts to exotic places, there were constant developments that clearly signaled groundbreaking change was on the cards for Australia's airlines and its aviation industry.

Since 1952 successive Australian governments had in place a two-airline policy. It meant the market was split between government-owned TAA and privately owned Ansett, each holding around 50% of the market. Neither could add aircraft or expand their networks without government permission, nor were they allowed to fly internationally. That was restricted to Qantas Airways, the Flying Kangaroo.

There was another smaller carrier, East-West Airlines, but it wasn't allowed to fly between major state capital cities so was confined to regional routes, and its ability to make inroads was severely restricted. Domestically, there was virtually no competition.

But by the middle of 1987, the Federal Labor Government, led by Prime Minister Bob Hawke, had declared aviation would be deregulated within three years.

That led to a scramble on all fronts. A deregulated industry would mean real competition, new entrant airlines. Lobbying began for all sorts of things. Ansett owner, Sir Reginald Ansett, wanted airlines to be allowed to purchase terminals at airports and operate them as their own. Air New Zealand indicated it wanted to operate domestically in Australia. Qantas wanted to operate domestically as well as internationally. TAA became Australian Airlines.

At the same time, Australia and the US constantly bickered over their air services agreement. These agreements were bilateral and laid down what routes an airline could fly between the two nations, what aircraft they could use, the number of seats they could offer, and the frequency of flights. After Australia refused to agree to an increase in flights for the American operator Continental Airlines, the US State Department blamed Canberra for 'a crisis in US-Australia aviation relations' and threatened to cut the number of flights Qantas could operate to the US. In the end, as usually happened, lengthy negotiations sorted things out.

All of this meant there continued to be a landslide of aviation stories, and it didn't end. The government introduced a $5 arrival fee for all incoming international passengers, which it expected airlines to collect.

The Board of Airline Representatives, which represented all the international airlines operating to and from Australia, rebelled, arguing they were being asked to act as tax collectors. It was disclosed 96,000 people had either failed or refused to pay the fee in one month, yet airlines were expected to make up the shortfall from their own budgets. Eventually, the government capitulated and removed the fee.

While the aviation landscape in Australia began to change, there were also diversions. American carrier United Airlines invited me to fly to Seattle to join a special flight, called Friendship One, arranged by a children's charity, the Friendship Foundation, to raise money. The aircraft was a Boeing B747 SP, or special performance. Shorter than the normal jumbo, it carried fewer passengers but could fly further.

The aim was to break the round-the-world speed record for a commercial flight. Of the 140 passengers, I was the only foreign journalist on board. Some had paid around $7,000 each for their seats.

Apart from five official pilots, there were 72 other aviators on board, including Neil Armstrong, the first man on the moon. He was one of the shyest people I have ever met, but happy to chat modestly about his achievements. During the flight he patiently posed with every passenger lined up for a photograph. I have always regretted that I didn't join the queue, but at least I was able to boast that I was one of the few people to have orbited the planet with Neil Armstrong. The flight took off from Seattle and flew to Athens, then on to Taipei, then back to Seattle. It had taken 36 hours, 54 minutes and 15 seconds, more than eight hours faster than had been done before.

On the news front, stories kept flowing. Stories about rising airfares; threatened industrial disputes at airports with air traffic controllers, who complained they were in despair, working with outdated equipment; ongoing bilateral squabbles over air rights, not only with the US but with Hong Kong and New Zealand.

Qantas and Cathay Pacific Airways were involved in an ongoing feud over whether there could be increases in capacity between Hong Kong and Australia.

The world's biggest jet, Russia's Antonov An-124, flew into a bicentennial air show at the RAAF base at Richmond, outside Sydney, but interviewing the crew was problematic. As soon as they parked the plane, they were off to enjoy the delights of Bondi Beach.

I was invited to join a flight on the supersonic Concorde on its Sydney to Perth leg. It had been chartered to fly a group of wealthy passengers around the world, the first supersonic circumnavigation of the earth. Because of the issues with the sonic boom, it couldn't fly over land, instead flying south, around Tasmania and across the Great Australian Bite. It took two hours and 45 minutes, compared to the four to five hours of normal commercial jets, flying at Mach 2, and reaching a cruising altitude of 60,000 ft, some 20,000 feet higher than other aircraft. From there you can see the curvature of the earth and feel you are almost in space.

There were more serious events. As United Airlines Flight 811 flew from Honolulu to Sydney, a cargo door partly opened in flight, ripping upwards and peeling off a large section of the fuselage in business class. This caused rapid decompression, during which seats, passengers, and interior fittings were sucked out into the airstream. Two Australians were among the nine people who died. All those killed were sitting on the right side of the cabin above the cargo door, and one was sucked into the engine. While the plane was carefully nursed back to Honolulu, where it landed safely, it was, of course, a big story in Sydney.

I wrote a feature that centered around concerns about the safety of ageing aircraft. The United plane, a B747-100, was built in 1970 and had flown for 58,800 hours, making 15,000 landings. The accident had been caused by a faulty latch on the cargo door.

Accompanying the article when it was published was a cartoon by Alan Moir. On the United jumbo depicted in the cartoon, the normal insignia on the tail had been replaced by the drawing of a hand with fingers crossed. The obvious suggestion was that if you were going to fly United, you had better cross your fingers and hope for the best. The airline's management in Chicago was not amused, and I was in their bad books, even though I told them pointedly I hadn't drawn the cartoon.

Soon, there was to be another record-breaking flight. Qantas had ordered ten Boeing B747-400s, the latest version of the jumbo jet. The first was to be delivered in August 1989. Normally, the delivery flight would have been from Seattle direct to the airline's base in Sydney.

Qantas had a different idea. It planned to fly it from Seattle to London and from there attempt something that had never been done before: operate a direct non-stop flight to Sydney.

Long-haul flying was a Qantas specialty, given Australia's geographic location. This would be groundbreaking. When Qantas helped establish what was called the Kangaroo Route in 1935, passengers traveling between England and Australia flew in five types of aircraft, owned by three airlines, and used two railways. There were 42 refueling stops, and the journey took between 12 and 14 days. A successful non-stop flight would not only be a huge publicity windfall, it would also add to the airline's reputation for long-haul flying.

I was invited to go to London and join the flight. Only 23 people boarded the plane, which would normally carry 376 passengers, four pilots (two captains and two First Officers), and cabin crew. On this flight, there were five pilots, commanded by Captain David Massey-Greene, as well as five other Qantas specialists and experts from Boeing and Rolls-Royce, whose engines powered the plane.

Because of weight restrictions crucial to the success of the flight, our luggage was returned to Sydney on a normal commercial service. Only 350 kg had been allowed for food and beverages, which meant rationing of drinks. The official drinks list included just two dozen cans of Foster's beer, not many for a 20-hour flight. There were five bottles of champagne, two bottles of white wine, and two of red, as well as various bottles of spirits.

Special jet fuel was brought by rail from Germany, and as we prepared for take-off, the aircraft didn't taxi to the end of the runway, it was towed there to save that little bit of extra fuel.

Arriving home after the Qantas record-breaking non-stop flight from London to Sydney. The airline's first Boeing B747-400 took 20 hours and nine minutes to cover the 17,850 km, August 16-17, 1989.

There was some concern about our passage over Continental Europe because air corridors were heavily congested, and flights were regularly moved around and delayed, but we needn't have worried. Aware of our mission, air traffic control cleared other traffic out of our way and sped us through, although at one stage, unexpected headwinds slowed our progress.

In case we ran out of fuel, alternative landing locations had been identified at Perth in WA and Adelaide in SA. They weren't required. By the time we crossed above the Australian coast at Carnarvon, we knew there was sufficient fuel.

When the plane, christened *City of Canberra*, touched down at Sydney's Kingsford Smith airport 20 hours and nine minutes after leaving London, it had broken a distance barrier that for years had seemed unbreakable.

As I write in 2023, there are still no non-stop commercial flights between London and Sydney, although Qantas does have non-stop flights from Perth to London using Boeing B787 Dreamliner aircraft. It has ordered 12 A350-1000 planes from Airbus, capable of Sydney–London non-stop, with these flights expected to begin in 2026.

The record-breaking non-stop flight may have been a highlight for Qantas, but Australia's domestic airlines were about to hit an all-time low.

The great Australian pilots dispute of late 1989 was probably the biggest aviation story I reported on for the SMH. The Australian Federation of Airline Pilots had been negotiating with Ansett, Australian Airlines, and East-West Airlines for months, arguing they had suffered a prolonged period of wage suppression. The union was campaigning for a 29.5% pay increase for its 1,640 domestic pilots and getting nowhere. In August, the pilots made themselves available for duty only between normal office hours of 9am to 5pm. Then the dispute worsened when pilots resigned en masse. Domestic air travel came to a grinding halt. It was nothing short of a crisis on a vast continent where air travel was vital to the economy.

Bob Hawke, now Prime Minister, declared a national emergency. This time the former union boss, famed for his ability to bring calm and negotiate settlements to disputes, inflamed matters by declaring the pilots were nothing more than 'glorified bus drivers'.

RAAF Hercules transport planes were brought in to operate some passenger services between major cities. The airlines chartered B737 and B757 aircraft from overseas airlines to fill some of the gaps. They were 'wet leased', which meant they came complete with cockpit and cabin crew. At the same time, pilots were being recruited overseas, in North America, Europe, Eastern Europe and elsewhere, slowly replacing the crew who had resigned. Some domestic passengers were even allowed to fly from Sydney to Perth via Singapore on Qantas international flights.

Inevitably, all of this led to serious questions about safety. It was hardly surprising that the grounded pilots and their union were accusing aviation authorities of rushing aircraft and foreign pilots into the air when they didn't meet normal Australian safety standards. But others were also concerned.

I wrote a front-page story with the headline: 'Air experts warn: "It's unsafe to fly"'. I interviewed Robert Greene, a former assistant director for operations in NSW of the Department of Transport. He declared many of Australia's high aviation standards had 'gone down the plughole'. And Roy Gray, a former examiner of pilots and expert of in-flight simulators with more than 123,000 hours flight time under his belt, said that despite denials, 'the desired level of safety has not and will not exist while the dispute follows its current path'. Both men said they would not fly under the present circumstances.

Flying a Boeing B747 simulator. Nearly every trip visiting an airline included an hour in one of their simulators. I was never a trained pilot, and my simulator landings were mostly shaky.

The Civil Aviation Authority rejected these claims, saying it would never permit any aircraft or crew to operate in Australian airspace unless they met the country's high air safety standards.

Nevertheless, it was clearly an issue. For one thing, regulations laid down that an aircraft carrying more than 44 people must be shown to be able to evacuate passengers and crew within 90 seconds. That criteria could not be met by the RAAF Hercules, which didn't have the required number of emergency exits.

And my contacts were telling me there had been incidents, such as when a French pilot who had entered the landing circuit at Sydney in the wrong direction, threatened the possibility of a head-on collision with aircraft flying in the right direction.

My writing about safety concerns came to a halt when the domestic airlines jointly applied for an injunction preventing me from reporting on this aspect of the dispute. It never reached court, but it had the desired effect, and I had to be very careful about what I wrote. It was the first and only time any sort of legal action has been taken against me in my entire career.

In the end, the dispute was never settled. By mid-December, the RAAF ceased its 'public transport operations', and the domestic airlines slowly began to get back to normal as they hired replacement pilots. As for the pilots who had resigned, many left the country to find positions with overseas airlines. Those who stayed could never again fly for Ansett or Australian, though some would find employment with the launch of new airlines after deregulation.

As a postscript to this, I flew to Zurich in Switzerland five months later, in May 1990, to interview 26 young pilots with Swissair – 24 of them had been with Australian Airlines. The bitterness was evident.

'They are Australians in exile. Angry young men given little choice, if they wanted to continue flying, but to leave their homeland and find new skies,' I wrote, adding, 'The future may not be so bleak for them, but the anger has not abated. Anger at the Prime Minister. Anger at Australia's domestic airlines. Anger at the media. Anger at a country that, they say, treated them 'like pariahs'.

They still declared Australia was home, but their feelings were clear. 'We may be here working but what about the others who are still at home out of a job?' one said. 'Planes may be flying but what happened in Australia will never be forgotten,' said another.

But there were mixed views among some pilots who had gone overseas. On that trip I also went to Munich in Germany, where six experienced pilots were now flying with charter airline LTU.

Captain Mark Reilly, a former Ansett pilot, said he wasn't bitter about what happened but still found it difficult to comprehend how the industry had allowed such a vast pool of experienced flying talent to disappear overseas. Ralph Young, another former Ansett pilot, said that in retrospect he thought the dispute might have been better led by the union. 'From my point of view one of the gripes was we handled it very poorly from an industrial and political point of view.'

It had, indeed, been a sad episode in Australia's aviation history.

14

Sky-high chaos

Deregulation of Australia's skies arrived at midnight on October 30, 1990. It ended those capacity controls that meant the market was shared 50/50 between Australian Airlines and Ansett as well as the number of aircraft they could operate. It also removed the requirement that airlines charge the same basic economy, business, and first-class fares, and controls over the importation of aircraft were also removed.

The market was opened to new entrants, and it didn't take long before they began to emerge. Compass said it would be Australia's first low-cost airline and would begin flying with a couple of leased jets by December. Transcontinental said it would have 12 Boeing B737s and would be flying by mid-1991. Southern Cross Airlines didn't give much detail of its plans but also suggested it would fly in 1991.

Best of all for air travelers, this dramatic change in the way Australia's airlines operated brought real competition to the market. It wasn't quite so good for the airlines. With the shackles of the two-airline policy removed, carriers began an all-out fight for market share, cutting fares and adding capacity. It meant their balance books took a hit and profits began to shrink, then became losses.

Neither was it good for any newcomer. Transcontinental never did get off the ground, and Southern Cross delayed its launch. Compass did fly but was out of business just a year after it launched.

The months leading up to deregulation and the years following were a golden age for an aviation writer with stories to tell daily. As the aviation editor of the prestigious *Sydney Morning Herald*, I was getting most of them ahead of competitors. Many were exclusive, although they weren't always to do with the new rules in the sky.

Just a month before deregulation arrived, I was tipped off about a near miss involving Qantas, known as one of the world's safest airlines. Qantas had suffered fatal accidents in the days of propellor-driven aircraft, but it had never suffered a fatal crash in the jet age. This one came very, very close.

The Qantas jumbo, flight QF10 from London to Sydney via Singapore, with 22 crew and 360 passengers, was flying over Thailand when it came within milliseconds of a mid-air collision with a giant US Air Force C-5 Galaxy transport jet. Traveling at a combined speed of 1,750 kph, they missed each other by only 17 meters. A mix-up involving Thai air traffic controllers had programmed them to converge at the same spot, 37,000 feet, or 12,000 meters, above Phuket at exactly the same time.

Technically, they should have collided. Avoidance of a disaster was a matter of pure chance, and it is likely a major catastrophe was averted only because of minor differences in the two aircrafts' instruments, such as the altimeter or automatic pilot. The Qantas pilot 'felt a bump as the airflow was disturbed, then he looked straight up and saw the back of the Galaxy going away toward the north,' the airlines flight operations line director and deputy chief pilot, Captain Roger Carmichael, told me at the time. Safety is always an airline's number-one priority, but it showed that, sometimes, it can also be a matter of pure luck.

My last few years at the SMH were a blur of activity. Story after story. The new airline that planned to launch as Southern Cross took on the brand of the collapsed Compass and took to the skies as Compass Mark 2. It didn't last even as long as its predecessor, failing after just six months, citing sustained fare discounting by its competitors as one of the main reasons.

East-West Airlines became a subsidiary of Ansett and soon disappeared altogether. The government put its domestic airline, Australian, up for sale. Qantas wanted to buy a share. The government said yes, then no, then yes again. In the end, Qantas bought the airline lock, stock, and barrel. The blue kangaroo began disappearing from the domestic airline's tails, replaced by Qantas's red kangaroo.

The merger was far from easy. The culture of the two carriers was dramatically different. Rationalization had to occur to eliminate positions that had doubled up. Qantas pilots saw themselves as superior to the former Australian Airlines pilots. When 'deadheading', traveling as passengers between posts to crew another flight, Qantas pilots insisted on being seated further forward in the plane than the Australian Airlines pilots. A feature I wrote headlined 'Turbulence Ahead – The troubled merger between Qantas and Australian' began:

> Just hours after Qantas announced earlier this month that Australian Airlines was to lose its name and have its planes repainted in Qantas colours, an official of the domestic carrier was asked how the news was being received. 'Pretty well', he replied. 'The staff are queuing up on the roof to take their turn at jumping off.' It may have seemed like black humour but it hid a deep-seated bitterness among Australian Airlines staff over their new owners and a yawning culture gap. Bridging the differences between the two airlines may be the toughest job management faces over the next six months.

Ultimately, it took years to truly merge the two airlines into a single Qantas international and domestic operation. And now that Qantas was flying domestically, Ansett complained it was at a disadvantage to its big rival. It wanted to fly internationally and was cleared to do so. It commenced international service on September 11, 1993, to Bali, followed by Osaka and Hong Kong in 1994, later adding Jakarta, Shanghai, Seoul, Taipei, and Kuala Lumpur.

Amid this, changes were taking place in management. Long-time Qantas chief executive John 'Tubby' Ward stepped down and was replaced by James Strong, who had been the CEO at the old Australian Airlines.

The aviation press corps called him Action Man. He looked like Barbie's Ken doll. Strong rode fast motorbikes, leathers and all. He went scuba diving, had even hitched a ride on a US Air Force plane to make a landing on an aircraft carrier. When Qantas invited a group of journalists to accompany him on the inauguration of a new route, he would challenge them to join him in the hotel gym for an exercise session at 6 am. I can't think of anyone who took him up on it; I certainly didn't.

These inaugural flights were something of a joyride, but they did give you the opportunity to chat with senior executives and get to know them better. When Qantas launched flights to Beijing, a side trip was organized to the Great Wall of China.

A unique experience took place in a Chinese jazz club. One of the guests on the flight was Ernie Dingo, Indigenous Australian actor, television presenter and comedian. There he was, on stage, jamming with the Chinese jazz musicians, playing the didgeridoo. I'm not sure how the Chinese saw it, but we thought it was great.

Back in Australia, another crisis involving aviation relations with the US American airline Northwest, which had been flying to Sydney from New York by way of Osaka, Japan. Australia acted, limiting the number of Japan–Australia passengers it could carry on these flights. The US retaliated by threatening to impose sanctions on Qantas's non-stop trans-Pacific flights to Los Angeles. It worsened when the US did stop Qantas flying to Los Angeles. But like most of these crises, the two sides eventually found a middle ground and a truce was declared.

At the Flying Kangaroo, there was another important change in the executive team. Ansett had a brilliant marketing director, a down-to-earth Australian, Geoff Dixon. He called me one day to meet him at a Sydney hotel that evening. We were sitting having a drink and chatting at a dimly lit table. The meeting was supposed to be secret but, as Murphy's Law would have it, in walked a woman who was a member of Ansett's public relations team. She wandered over to say hullo and asked, 'What are you two up to?' Dixon replied, 'Oh, we're just having a friendly chat'.

In fact, he was telling me that he had come to meet me direct from a meeting with James Strong at Qantas. He was going to leave Ansett and join its rival, something I was able to report exclusively the following day.

It was no accident that when Dixon was at Ansett, it always seemed to have the upper hand over Qantas. After he joined Qantas, the tables were turned. It was Dixon who pinned down the rights to use *I Still Call Australia Home*, a song written by Peter Allen in 1980 that tells of Australian expatriates' longing for home, as the theme for an advertising campaign that would become the airline's best ever. Dixon was later to take over from Strong as Qantas chief executive.

There was the odd, unusual assignment. I had the crazy idea of writing a feature on what it was like to be a flight attendant. I thought I'd just dress up as cabin crew and do a short domestic hop with Qantas, but it was not quite so easy. The airline agreed but said they couldn't let me loose on their passengers unless I completed the eight-week cabin crew training course. This I did, as well as continuing to write news stories in between. The final two weeks of the course were dedicated to emergency procedures (Eps). You had to get a minimum of 94 out of 100 to pass, and if you didn't pass, you didn't fly. I succeeded and had a Qantas certificate to prove it.

Having gone to the trouble of going through this grueling procedure, I was ready to fly. It wasn't to be on any brief domestic hop.

'You need to do the loop,' the airline said. The loop? 'It's the toughest long-haul route in the world. It'll take eight days and by the end of it you'll really know what it's like to be a flight attendant,' they explained. The route was Sydney to Bangkok to London and back, with crew layovers in Thailand and the UK.

As it turned out, it wasn't quite as straightforward as that. London was fogged in, and if we left Bangkok on time, we wouldn't be able to land at London's Heathrow Airport. The captain decided to leave on time anyway but fly to Bahrain in the Middle East, stop there, refuel, then go on to London, by which time it was forecast the fog would have cleared. It turned what should have been a 14-hour flight into one that took more than 18 hours.

I certainly found out what it really was like to be cabin crew. It was hard work. Dealing with 400 passengers, feeding them, plying them with drinks, handling those who had imbibed far too much, always smiling, and always looking like a catwalk model. Do you know how many cupboards, receptacles, drawers, and hidden corners there are on a Boeing B747?

This Qantas flight carried 28,000 items to meet passenger needs. Everything from playing cards to knives and forks, meals, baby food, nappies, pens, deodorant spray, first-aid kits, scissors, alcohol, and blankets. On Qantas, there were even individual servings of Vegemite. The plane is an absolute maze of hidden nooks and crannies, and as a flight attendant, you must remember them all. But in the end, it was worth it. The experience produced a great feature.

Of course, there were many other stories. Airlines making huge profits, then dreadful losses. The ongoing marketing battle between Qantas and Ansett. Controversy over construction of a third runway at Sydney Airport. Orders for new aircraft. More industrial disputes involving airline and airport staff, as well as air traffic controllers. The privatization of government-owned Qantas. Congestion in the air and on the ground. A decades-long debate over whether

Sydney needed a second airport and, if so, where it should be, was a hot topic.

In 1994 the Federal Government decided to fast-track the building of the second airport at Badgerys Creek, in Western Sydney. It would be built by 1996, it said. In a comment piece headlined 'Fast-tracking to cloud cuckoo land', I wrote:

> Anyone who believes there will be a viable international airport at Badgerys Creek by 1996, as reported by some parts of the media yesterday, is living in cloud cuckoo land. That isn't a stab in the dark. It is a fact of life. For if Badgerys Creek is turned from green farmland into a modern aviation facility in such a short time, it will be one of the greatest miracles in the history of the airline industry.

I was right. It didn't happen, though the construction now, in 2023, is finally underway, with a scheduled opening in 2026.

Other things were happening in my career around this time that were to play an important role in where I was heading. While still at the SMH, I was also writing for a major aviation magazine in London, *Airline Business*, which had asked me to be one of their correspondents in the Asia–Pacific region. Then, while attending an aviation conference in Bangkok, I met Barry Grindrod, co-publisher with his wife Christine McGee of a new magazine called *Orient Aviation*, published in Hong Kong.

Barry was English, Christine, Australian, and they had both been writing for newspapers in Hong Kong before deciding to launch the magazine, which was published every two months. Barry asked me if I could interview Qantas's James Strong for the magazine, which I duly did. After that, I continued to contribute various stories.

Then, things changed at the SMH: a new editor, John Alexander, and a push to severely trim the budget and rationalize operations across the board. One day, Alexander called me into his office and explained they wanted me to become a sort of mega-transport editor, covering not only aviation but shipping, rail, road transport, and anything else with wheels, basically. Clearly, they were trying to cut staff numbers. Topics that had previously been covered by two or three separate rounds of people were now to be covered by one.

I didn't even have to think about it. Now a deeply committed specialist writing on all things to do with aviation, I had no interest in ships, or trains, or anything else. I wouldn't do it.

'Well', said Alexander, 'we'll find someone else who will'. The washup from this was my departure, though I wouldn't be simply walking out the door with nothing. They offered me a redundancy package, a lump sum payment to leave. As well as that, I was owed several thousand dollars in pay for weeks of holidays which I hadn't used.

Strangely, I wasn't angry or downhearted. I had been at the SMH for a wonderful 18 years, transforming myself from an all-round general reporter, bureau chief, and chief of staff into a recognized specialist on aviation. Whatever happened next, that was what I'd be for the rest of my career.

15

Footloose and fancy-free

Taking stock, I pondered where I was now, a freelance journalist. My own boss. It can be a fragile business, finding new customers who want what you write, but I had a head start. I was already contributing to *Airline Business* in London and *Orient Aviation* in Hong Kong, and I had a solid reputation as a specialist writer on aviation matters. Who else? I needn't have worried.

The terms of my redundancy ruled I could not contribute to the SMH. However, I was able to write for another Fairfax publication, the *Australian Financial Review*. It carried regular special reports and surveys on various issues or countries. I was invited to contribute. If, for example, there was a special report on Japan, I would write a story about Japan's airlines or a new airport that was being built. There were plenty of business stories relating to aviation, such as how airlines were making lots of money with their frequent flyer schemes, or how they were upgrading business and first-class lounges to lure executive travelers. The battle to capture business flyers, who mostly paid big money to sit at the front of the plane, was fierce.

The *Australian Financial Review* wasn't my only new outlet. *The Australian*, major rival to the SMH, also took me on board, and I began writing regular news stories and features for them.

Then there was *The Bulletin* magazine, where I became a regular contributor. One cover story I did for them was an exclusive interview with Qantas CEO James Strong. It followed an accident involving one of the airline's Boeing B747s, which had landed at Bangkok's Don Muang airport in a thunderstorm but couldn't stop.

It ran off the end of the runway, collided with a ground antenna, smashing the front undercarriage, and ending up with its nose resting on a perimeter road. None of the 391 passengers, 16 cabin crew, and three pilots were injured, but it put a dent in the carrier's reputation as one of the world's safest airlines.

Qantas didn't normally talk about its great safety record, aware that a good safety reputation is a fragile asset. But Strong agreed to talk to me. Qantas was a tall poppy and a natural target. Critics began questioning the airline's standards, suggesting micromanagement of the business could be placing unprecedented pressure on staff and that the drive for bigger profits might be narrowing the safety–comfort zone.

The Bulletin cover had a photograph of the Qantas jumbo stuck at the airport perimeter with a headline asking,

'Is QANTAS Safe?' Inside, the story had a photograph of Strong with the banner 'High Anxiety'. He strongly refuted the criticisms.

'Qantas still observes standards which are above the required minimum in virtually every area of our operation – including maintenance and safety issues', he insisted.

Qantas public relations also invited me to write articles for their in-flight magazine *The Australian Way*. One was about a flight aboard a jumbo jet leased by a travel company to operate sightseeing flights over Antarctica. Roz joined me as we took off from Sydney, flew four hours south to the frozen continent, spent four hours flying over this incredible land, then four hours back to Sydney. It was, officially, a domestic flight because it took off and landed at an Australian airport.

On another occasion, the airline flew me to New Zealand and arranged a rental car for me to drive around and write a piece about a motoring holiday on the country's South Island.

There was more serious and detailed writing. The *Economist Intelligence Unit* in London began asking me to contribute to their travel and tourism reports on various aspects of airline and airport operations in Asia–Pacific, as well as tourism. In 1997, I wrote a research report for them, *The Airline Industry in Asia – Corporate strategies and market prospects*.

It was a huge task, including chapters on the place of Asian airlines on the world stage, demographic and social influences, and Asia's impact on the international travel industry, profiles on every major airline in the region, airline strategies, infrastructure and key issues, fleet growth and investment prospects, as well as prospects and conclusions. The report ended up being a 311-page volume that told you everything you needed to know about the region's airline and aviation industry.

This was a period during which the world was awakening to the fact that the center of gravity of aviation was moving eastwards. Air traffic in the region was beginning to overtake the historical dominance of Europe and North America. The middle classes in Asia were emerging in growing numbers in places like India, China, Japan, and Korea. They wanted to travel, and low-cost airlines were beginning to give birth to a new airline sector that made it affordable to them.

It was also a time when there was another twist in my career path. Barry from *Orient Aviation* called me to ask if I would consider writing exclusively for them. In return, I would be appointed chief correspondent and be given a 5 per cent stake in the magazine, which was published under the parent company, Wilson Press. I would still, officially, be freelance and be paid not a regular salary, but a certain amount for each printed word. Since I ended up writing most of the magazine, it was a pretty good deal. I contacted *Airline Business* in London, explained the situation, and apologized, departing their fold amiably.

Writing for *Orient Aviation* took me into a different world. At the SMH much of what I was doing was parochially Australian. As a freelancer, my landscape had widened and much of Asia was my patch. Now, it was to broaden onto the world stage.

The growing focus on Asia had me adding another string to my bow. I was regularly asked to appear on Australian television shows to talk about airline matters. As well as this, international news services, mainly CNN and Al Jazeera, called on me to appear and discuss events not only in Asia.

If there was an air crash in South America, Europe or elsewhere, they would ask me on to speculate on the causes. I say 'speculate' because air-crash investigations take months, even years, to complete and talking about them a day after they've happened can be tricky. Fortunately, with the arrival of rapid communication through the internet and fast news, you could quickly catch up with some of the circumstances involved in a crash. Was it in bad weather? Were there witnesses, and what did they see? Could terrorism be involved? Could there have been a mechanical issue with the plane? What kind of safety record did the airline have?

All of these and more had to be considered. It was good for my image, but it was also good for the magazine because each time I appeared, I was introduced as the Chief Correspondent of *Orient Aviation* magazine. It put the brand before a global audience.

I had already traveled extensively, but working for the magazine added many more air miles to my record. There were visits to the aircraft manufacturers, Boeing in Seattle, Airbus in Toulouse, as well as Embraer in Brazil.

Aviation writers from around the globe during a Boeing media tour at the aircraft manufacturer's Seattle base. I'm second from the left.

Then there were the jet-engine makers, such as Rolls-Royce in Derby, England. Each year we had a team attend the big air shows, one year in Paris, the next at Farnborough in the UK. The magazine had its own stand at each, though we eventually stopped that because it became too expensive.

The air shows were tiring because everything was spread out, and you had to trek back and forward all the time, usually in summer heat. But they did give you the opportunity to have face-to-face meetings with senior airline and industry executives. And the big companies all had chalets where they entertained guests with lavish amounts of food and drink. As you might imagine, the aviation press spent much time enjoying the entertainment.

But there were times when life's ups and downs interrupted proceedings. Roz came to London with me one year, when I was attending the Farnborough Air Show. Orient Aviation had rented a house in the city for the team to stay for the duration.

We were only there for one day when Roz's sister Elaine phoned with the sad news that their mother had passed away. I immediately called Qantas in London to arrange a flight home but was having trouble getting anything done, so I called the Qantas head of public relations (PR) in Sydney, Jim Eames, and explained the situation. We were on the next Qantas flight back to Sydney – one of the benefits of being a well-known aviation writer.

At the Paris Air Show at Le Bourget in 1989 with Airbus's Australian corporate communications head, Ted Porter.

At one Paris air show, we went from the airport to the show directly to set up our stand, and then grabbed a taxi to take us to the hotel in central Paris. When we arrived, it was discovered that our publisher, Christine McGee, had left her suitcase behind. It had apparently not been loaded into the taxi but left by the side of the road. An urgent phone call was made to one of our advertising executives who was still at the show asking him to track it down. He did, but it was bad news.

'The gendarmes found it but because they didn't know who it belonged to or what was in it, they exploded it,' he explained.

This was a disaster for Christine, but we couldn't ignore the funny side, an image of her frilly underwear being blown up and floating in all directions around the show. She had to go out the next day and do some emergency clothes-shopping, which probably ended up being a bonus for her.

At another air show, this time Farnborough in the UK, I had another one of those triumphant moments. A few months earlier I had traveled to the US to dig into a story about America's drive to forge open-skies agreements with all and sundry. These were air service deals that were exactly what they sounded like. Open skies meant no limitations on the number of flights or destinations between two countries.

Some thought it was a good idea. Others were strongly averse, fearing their own international airlines would be overrun by the big American majors like United, Delta and American. I traveled around talking to airline chiefs and to Washington, where I interviewed senators, congressmen, and government aviation officials to get a good understanding of their thinking and determine exactly how their open-skies campaign was progressing.

The piece I wrote was a cover story in *Orient Aviation*, and during a gala dinner at London's Hilton Hotel, it was announced it had won me the GE Aircraft Engines award for the Best Air Transport Submission in the Royal Aerospace Society's Aerospace Journalist of the Year Awards, 1998. Accepting the award in front of hundreds of executives from the world's airline and aviation industry was a career highlight and, of course, a big boost for the magazine itself. It cemented the publication's place and its writers as leading players on the global aviation media scene.

Receiving the Royal Aerospace Society award at a gala dinner in London as Aerospace Journalist of the Year in 1998.

It wasn't the last award I was to receive. In 2000, despite the fact I was writing for a Hong Kong-published magazine, I was named Australia's aviation journalist of the year. I also won the award for the best aviation feature story of the year, an honor which I was to receive five more times in the ensuing years.

Of course, awards are an ego thing. But they are also important because they were voted on by your peers and people from the aviation industry. They show that what you are doing is being recognized, and they boost your confidence.

Key annual events had to be covered, which also involved a lot of travel. The IATA Annual General Meeting and Aviation Summit, hosted in a different country by a member airline, was held in June each year.

To name a few of the locations we visited: Berlin, hosted by Lufthansa; Cancun with Aero Mexico; Miami Beach with Delta Airlines; Beijing with Air China; Sydney with Qantas; and Qatar with Qatar Airways. These gatherings were important because everyone who was anyone in the industry, from airlines to airports, aircraft and engine manufacturers, aircraft lessors, industry analysts and others, attended. In three or four days, you could gather enough stories to keep you going for months.

IATA was a key source for us. It represented all the world's airlines, and it could provide experts in almost any area of the industry for comment on issues. It also had a great public relations team led by Tony Concil, Vice-President for Corporate Communications, in Geneva. I first met him when he was assistant manager, international public relations, at Japan's All Nippon Airways. A Canadian, he spoke fluent Japanese. Then, in the region, Albert Tjoeng led the PR team in Singapore. It didn't seem to matter what time of the day or night you emailed Albert, he would invariably answer almost immediately.

When I first had dealings with IATA, it was very much a northern hemisphere-centric organization, regarded by many as a sort of retirement home for ageing aviation industry figures.

That all changed in 2002 when Giovanni Bisignani, the Italian dynamo, became director general. A former CEO of Italy's national airline Alitalia, he completely reorganized IATA and turned much of his attention to Asia, which was clearly becoming the growth engine of the industry. He was outspoken, sometimes controversial, and delighted in attacking airports, accusing them of overcharging airlines for their services. He often started speeches with a loud cry of *Basta!*, an Italian word that essentially means 'enough is enough'.

He was succeeded in 2011 by Tony Tyler, a former CEO of Cathay Pacific Airways, and a good friend of *Orient Aviation*. He was the first IATA director general to come from the Asia–Pacific region. As he approached the end of his five-year tenure in 2015, I contacted Tony Concil and asked if an interview could be arranged to talk about Tony Tyler's time as director general.

Tony came back with the surprising suggestion: 'Why don't you do it in Cuba?' CUBA! The airline body was founded in Havana in April 1945, when 57 airlines gathered in the city's Hotel Nacional. To celebrate IATA's 70th anniversary, Tyler was going to Havana to host a dinner at the hotel, in the very room where it had begun life.

It was Damascus all over again. The question for me was: How the hell do I get there? Where do I get a visa? Cuba was still an isolated nation. No Australian or American airlines flew there, but Air Canada did. IATA booked me a business-class ticket from Sydney to Vancouver, on to Montreal, and down to Havana.

As for the visa, it was far simpler than I thought. You didn't have to get one in advance. When you board the Air Canada flight in Montreal, cabin crew hand out a visa form to be filled in, and it was issued on arrival in Havana. However, I had to go to the Ministry of Information to get an official foreign media pass.

As expected, Cuba was like stepping back into the 1950s, with old classic cars in abundance. Havana looked a little rundown in places, but the people were friendly, despite their isolation in a Communist state. They talked easily about their life, things that were in short supply, and how they would love to be open to the whole world. As I have found everywhere, these ordinary people just wanted a good, healthy existence, and to be at peace. The 70th anniversary dinner was, of course, a great success and I had my interview with Tony Tyler.

Like IATA, the Association of Asia-Pacific Airlines (AAPA) Assembly of Presidents hosted a gathering each year in November at the home base of a different Asian airline. Given our focus on the region it was, again, the perfect opportunity to interview chief executives and hear about the challenges they were facing. In early December, IATA held its Global Media Days at its head office in Geneva, Switzerland. Aviation writers from around the world were flown in for two days of detailed briefings on every aspect of the industry.

In December 2009, on my way to Switzerland to attend that event, I received some bad news. I was getting ready to board my flight to Geneva when there was a phone call. My mother was gravely ill in Dundee hospital. Both my parents had been in the Balhousie Pitlochry Care Home for several years. We had chosen it over some anonymous facility in Edinburgh because it was in a pleasant setting, surrounded by trees and close to the River Tay. The only difficulty was that I lived in Australia and my sister lived in the US. Luckily, we had wonderful relatives in Pitlochry, Peter Rae, my cousin, and his wife Sheena. Sheena had been a nurse and kept an eye on them for us, updating us on how things were going. She called me in London, saying my mother wasn't expected to last the night.

After calling IATA to explain the situation, I quickly arranged to get on a flight to Edinburgh, where I collected a rental car and drove to Dundee. When I got there, she was still alive, but I almost didn't recognize her. She was skeletal and clearly not aware of anything around her, but the important thing was that I had made it. I was there by her side when she passed away.

At her cremation, the music we chose was Scotland's unofficial national anthem, *Flower of Scotland*, which is exactly what she was. My father passed away almost a year later.

A few months later, we were in Scotland on a visit. Roz and I, my sister who had come from America, and several of our relations took their ashes up into the hills, to the two-up, two-down cottage where Mum had been brought up and where we had all spent so many happy times. We spread the ashes in the nearby burn where we once collected buckets of water. It eventually flowed into the Tay. Just think, I quipped later, every time you eat some salmon from the Tay you might be getting a tiny bit of Mum and Dad.

Back at work, both IATA and AAPA invited me to moderate chief executive panels during their events. They were lots of fun. Conducted before an audience of hundreds, usually you would have four or five airline CEOs that you could quiz, asking them to talk about issues, answer controversial questions, and invite delegates to ask their own questions from the floor. They always ended up providing lively, interesting stories.

Various trips were organized by Boeing and Airbus. For example, Boeing had a two-week media tour each year, flying in journalists from around the world, during which time you visited Seattle, where it built commercial aircraft; St Louis, Missouri, home of its military manufacturing; and Long Beach, California, where some of its space operations took place. For me, much of this was a waste of time since I was only interested in the commercial side of the business, not defense or space.

Airbus would have annual gatherings at its base in Toulouse, France, to update everyone on new developments. It also invited me to China, where it had begun completion work on its aircraft being delivered to Chinese airlines at Tianjin. This involved basic A320 aircraft being flown to China and fitted out there. On the same trip I was flown to Harbin in Northern China, where an Airbus facility produced parts for its aircraft.

At our headquarters office in Hong Kong was a significant change: Barry and Christine had divorced. Barry eventually went back to England, leaving Christine to shoulder the entire burden of publishing the magazine and keeping it going. It was something she was to do with singular purpose over ensuing years, often in the face of great adversity.

On the publishing side, I wasn't of much assistance. I was a writer and had never edited. All I could do was continue to provide a flow of good copy. And I had an addition to my title, now being associate editor and chief correspondent.

16

Extraordinary leaders

A memoir or autobiography is about one's life and experiences, but individuals don't live in isolation. Your beliefs, the way you act, behave and approach life are molded by your parents, your teachers, things you see, and the people you meet – people you learn from and admire. In my career I've been fortunate to have met and interviewed some extraordinary men. I say *men* because only a handful of women are in charge of airlines around the world. It is something the industry is aware of and is working to correct.

At *Orient Aviation* we carried monthly special reports on subjects such as maintenance, repair and overhaul (or MRO), aircraft and engine leasing, airports, air traffic control, and other aspects of the industry. My main task each month was to interview an airline chief executive, not only in the Asia–Pacific but in the Gulf, India, Europe, or North America. In more than a quarter century with the magazine, I've conducted hundreds of exclusive interviews with airline chiefs.

Not all the interviews went smoothly. After flying to Hanoi to interview the CEO of Vietnam Airlines, the airline called me at my hotel to say the meeting had to be postponed for two days because he'd had to fly to Ho Chi Minh City, the old Saigon, on urgent business. Not to worry … a time to play tourist.

Hanoi is an interesting place, its architecture a reflection of its French colonial days. From my hotel room, I could see the Hanoi Opera House, built by the French colonial administration between 1901 and 1911. It could have been lifted straight from Central Paris. Just five minutes' walk away was Hoan Kiam Lake, with the ancient Turtle Tower perched on a tiny island in the middle. There you can sit at a lakeside café and watch the world go by.

Another call from the airline. They apologized, but the interview had to be canceled. The CEO had now flown overseas, again on urgent business. So, it was back to Sydney with a blank tape recorder. But all was not lost. We agreed I would email a list of questions, and they would email me back his responses. This duly done, the cover story on Vietnam Airlines and its CEO eventually came to pass.

Before the COVID-19 pandemic struck in earnest in early 2020 – and more of that later – these interviews were conducted face-to-face. An airline would fly me to their home base, where I would have a one-to-two-hour chat covering every aspect of the airline's operations, from fleet and network growth to its financial situation and the challenges that lay ahead.

I described some of those men as extraordinary, and that's because they work in an extraordinary industry and often must make extraordinary decisions. Running an airline is one of the world's most complex businesses. Their assets, the aircraft, cost billions of dollars. CEOs and management must make decisions on which routes to fly. Will they be profitable? If not now, soon?

They must deal with a myriad of regulations differing from destination to destination; keep their passengers happy with in-flight services that must be constantly updated; and ensure an adequate workforce, a certain number of pilots for each plane they operate and sufficient engineers to maintain them.

They must deal with airports, negotiate take-off and landing slots, and work out how much to charge for each seat to ensure profitability. The complexity is endless.

Over the years, the airline industry has often been a chronic basket case. While there are a few outstanding examples of carriers that do make good money – and many of those operate in the Asia–Pacific region – the fiscal record of the airline industry is woeful. In the first decade of the 21st century, the world's airlines jointly lost more than $50 billion.

Their business history is one of boom and bust, with endless cycles of oversupply and undersupply, of rash competitive traits that meant they self-destructed through vicious bouts of price-cutting that, in some cases, even led to their primary product, the airline seat, being given away for less than the cost of producing it. And many of the things that impact their fortunes are totally outside their control, such as severe weather, the cost of jet fuel, politics, and even conflicts, such as Russia's war in Ukraine.

An anecdote is often told at aviation industry conferences by speakers attempting to instill a little ironic humor into their presentations. It concerns the world's most successful investor, American multi-billionaire Warren Buffet, and a comment he famously made in a 2002 interview.

Buffet, so the story goes, suggested that if he had been around in the early 1900s when Orville and Wilbur Wright were launching their frail biplane into the skies from the sand dunes at Kittyhawk in Louisiana for the first time, he would have grabbed a ground-to-air missile launcher and blasted it out of the air. This would have saved a lot of investors a great deal of money over the years to come.

That version of the story isn't quite accurate, though it is not far from the truth. What Buffett really said was that if a capitalist had been present at Kittyhawk, he should have shot Orville Wright, who piloted the maiden flight of the Wright Flyer, thereby opening the age of powered flight. Why? Buffett described the airline business as extraordinary.

> It has eaten up capital over the past century like almost no other business because people seem to keep coming back to it and putting fresh money in. You've got huge, fixed costs, you've got strong

labor unions and you've got commodity pricing.
That is not a great recipe for success.

Buffett went on to add, 'I have an 800 number now that I call if I get the urge to buy an airline stock. I call at two in the morning, and I say: 'My name is Warren and I'm an aeroholic.' And then they talk me down.'

So why then do airlines attract those special people who normally stick with it for life, despite the challenges? I can't write about all the airline chiefs that I have interviewed, but a few stand out, such as Rod Eddington, who was born in Perth, WA. He graduated from the University of WA with a Master of Engineering degree, and in 1974, was the Rhodes Scholar from WA, enabling him to complete his Doctorate of Philosophy (DPhil) in the Department of Engineering Science at Oxford University.

He joined the Swire Group, which owned Cathay Pacific in Hong Kong, where I first met him. At the time, Rod was marketing director at Cathay, but he later became the airline's chief executive. After leaving Cathay, he became executive chairman of Ansett Australia, then moved on to become chief executive of British Airways.

Rod liked Australian friends visiting London to drop in and see him. His driver would come to the hotel and pick you up to take you to BA headquarters. In 2005, he was knighted for services to the British transport industry, becoming Sir Roderick Eddington, but it is a mark of the man that afterwards, his business card did not contain the word 'Sir', just a simple 'Rod Eddington'. And he insisted he should still be addressed as 'plain old Rod'. I call him 'the man who killed Concorde' because it was he who took the decision to finally ground the supersonic jet.

One thing Concorde did have was a perfect safety record ... until July 25, 2000, when Air France flight AF 4590 plunged in a ball of flame into the French countryside shortly after take-off from Paris's Charles de Gaulle international airport. This horrendous crash, seen by numerous eyewitnesses, resulted in the deaths of 113 passengers and crew. During its take-off run, a tire had struck a piece of debris on the runway, causing it to burst. Flying chunks of rubber punctured a fuel tank, causing a leak and subsequent engine fire.

After being retrofitted with Kevlar fuel tank liners and improved tires, the Concorde fleet took to the skies again in November 2001, but the timing could hardly have been worse. Just two months earlier, on September 9, 2001, two commercial aircraft destroyed New York's Twin Towers – the World Trade Center – and smashed into a section of the Pentagon in Washington. A third aircraft, which the terrorists had hoped to fly into the Capitol Building in Washington, crashed in Pennsylvania after passengers attempted to intervene in the terrorist plans. Those 9/11 attacks sparked a massive downturn in air travel markets, fuel was becoming more and more expensive, and the 30-year-old Concorde needed increasing maintenance to keep it flying.

Air France soon ceased Concorde operations, but BA soldiered on for a while. The last Concorde commercial flight, a BA service, left New York's John F Kennedy airport and landed in London on October 23, 2003, ending the era of supersonic passenger flight.

Talking to me about the day he finally grounded an aviation icon, Eddington said the great tragedy in the ultimate demise of Concorde was not that it had to be retired.

'The great tragedy is actually we haven't been able to find a son or daughter of Concorde. That technology has not yet reached a stage where we can build an airplane that can fly supersonically and is viable in economic terms.'

Eddington said it was 'a very difficult decision emotionally' but that for many people at the airline 'there was a view that, sad as it was, it was on balance the right thing to do'. Operating Concorde had become unviable in an economic sense. He said it was an airplane designed in the 1960s and built in the 1970s in a very different technological world. Keeping an airplane operating 30 or 40 years after it was built was a real challenge.

> You can do it, but in order to do it safely, you need to invest more and more money in that airframe. It is one of the things that impacted on Concorde's operating economics, the cost of maintenance and keeping it in the air. The balance of these two things – what happened on the demand side and the increased cost of keeping it

> running – meant that Concorde reached a point in its journey where it had to be retired. That happened on my watch and ultimately, I, as chief executive, took responsibility for that.

Another amazing person I interviewed was Idris Jala, a descendant of the Kelabit, an Indigenous people of the Bario Highlands in Northern Sarawak, part of the Malaysian state of Borneo. Little more than a century previously, the wiry men of this jungle people were involved in head-hunting raids, mainly as a means of proving individual courage and bravery. That was ancient history, and Idris was a senior executive with the Shell oil company, persuaded by the Malaysian Government to take charge of its ailing national carrier, Malaysia Airlines (MAS), which was losing hundreds of millions of dollars annually.

A few months after he took over in December 2005, I met him in the plush lobby of Le Meridien Montparnasse Hotel in Paris, where he was attending IATA's 62nd AGM. After introducing myself, I asked if we could sit down and have a chat. He didn't hesitate.

'No problem,' he responded. This was to be no official boardroom interview, but a casual, relaxed, and friendly chat, sitting around a coffee table in the hotel lobby. Although I didn't know it at the time, it was the beginning of a remarkable story of airline management. This affable, always smiling Malaysian executive had not only taken charge of an airline, but had also inherited a corporate disaster.

When Idris took over, the carrier had only three months of operating cash in its coffers. It had lost $352.5 million in the nine months ending December 31, 2005, and was heading for a further deficit of $461 million in the 12 months ending December 31, 2006.

Idris had absolutely no airline industry experience, but during that first interview in Paris, one thing very quickly became clear; the knowledge he had amassed on the intricacies of running an airline in just a few months was astounding.

Questioned by a journalist who had spent 20 years covering every aspect of aviation and airline operations, he fielded each inquiry with incredible ease and a supreme mastery of the subject. So how did this newcomer to airlines ultimately perform?

At the end of 2007, just two years after becoming CEO, MAS had risen from the ashes of near-bankruptcy to report its highest-ever profit in 60 years of operations, income of $283 million. How did he do it? It was a textbook example of financial turnaround in the airline industry. After taking charge, he quickly identified the four key areas causing problems. The first was low yield; the second, an inefficient network; the third, low productivity because of too many staff; and the fourth, poor control over costs.

Idris took off the kid gloves and started to work hard and fast. In a bid to reduce costs dramatically and improve yields, he slashed jobs – staff numbers were reduced from 22,700 to 19,000 – and cut routes. He realized any hope of success hinged on two critical issues, reducing costs, and increasing yields. To achieve the first, he did the expected. He set out on a relentless drive to re-engineer the business, trim expenses across the board, increase productivity, and rationalize the network.

To tackle the second, he did the unexpected. In an industry heavily reliant on sophisticated information technology systems to cope with every aspect of the business, he turned off the computer that ran the carrier's pricing structure and seat inventory and did it his way.

Why? Jala had a theory that the network revenue management systems used by airlines to cope with the industry's incredibly complex fare structure were perpetuating low yields:

> There is probably no other industry anywhere in the world that has a pricing mechanism as complex as the airlines. If you have 118 routes, as we do, there are something like 2.5 million fare permutations and these are changing daily.

That is why, he explained, every airline today runs its pricing structure and seat inventory through sophisticated IT systems.

But Jala backed his judgment and formed a team whose job was to take the system offline and produce massive spreadsheets covering every route the carrier operated. They had to look at 2.5 million fares daily, compare them with competitors, and manually adjust them to ensure they were competitive. It was a massive task, but his team persisted. The proof came on the bottom line. When Jala took the helm, passenger yields were US cents 6.5 per revenue passenger-kilometer. By the end of September 2006, they were US cents 8.4 per RPK (revenue passenger kilometers). By the end of March 2007, they were at US cents 8.7.

He had six commandments that might well be adopted by all airline chief executives. They were:

- The game of the impossible. You must do things everybody says cannot be done.

- Everything you do must be anchored on the P & L, the company's profit and loss.

- Discipline. The entire organization must be disciplined in what is being done, and action-orientated with it. *Don't think about it, do it.*

- Leadership. At the beginning of the journey as a leader you need to be highly directive. It's not a democracy. You must take charge. In a war you can have only one general... you tell people what you want to do and once they figure out how to do it, you start to empower them. Empowerment starts in the latter part but not in the beginning.

- Create a winning coalition. You must work with the government, the shareholders, the unions, employees, and all interested parties to get them on board by engaging and being transparent.

- Divine intervention. Some 60% of what happens to us we cannot control. We only control 40%. However good you are, the day you think the world is at your feet is the day you will crumble. Humility is a virtue. We can't control the oil price or the financial crisis... I am totally acutely aware that whatever we did, if events did not work in our favor, we could still fail. You must accept that vulnerability is a virtue.

Being based in Australia, I've obviously had plenty of contact with Qantas chief executives. If ever an airline has had a great run with chiefs, it is the Flying Kangaroo. From James Strong to Geoff Dixon and his successor Alan Joyce, they have all been consummate operators, prepared to take the hard, and sometimes risky, decisions.

In 2004, when Dixon launched low-cost Jetstar – the name was suggested by his daughter – there was almost unanimous belief the move was madness. A full-service airline like Qantas should stick to what it knows, they said. The decision was part of a new, two-brand strategy, with Qantas competing at the high end of the market and Jetstar competing with Australia's first successful LCC, Virgin Blue. Despite the critics, it worked.

Jetstar grew quickly and was soon flying internationally, as well as having subsidiaries, such as Jetstar Asia in Singapore, Jetstar Japan, and Jetstar Pacific in Vietnam. As I've said before, the trend for full-service airlines across the region to launch their own LCC subsidiaries spread quickly, becoming a permanent part of the airline landscape.

Alan Joyce, who had been chief executive of Jetstar before taking over from Dixon at Qantas, was born in Ireland, and had originally worked with Aer Lingus before coming to Australia in 1996 to join Ansett, before moving to Qantas in 2000. He was a hard-nosed businessman. With the media he was amiable, chatty, and often wandered into the bar to drink with you. He was also prepared to take tough decisions.

In late 2011, Qantas was hit by a number of industrial disputes over the bargaining of new enterprise agreements with various unions. Engineers, pilots, and baggage handlers carried out various industrial actions, including work stoppages. With the Christmas and New Year holiday period approaching, the airline's busiest time, and unions threatening further disruption to cause holiday chaos, Joyce acted. He grounded the entire airline, at home and abroad.

All Qantas aircraft already on the ground, regardless of whether they were in maintenance or serviceable, were grounded, and all passengers who had boarded aircraft were instructed to disembark and collect their baggage. Some aircraft turned around during taxiing for take-off, and flights that were in the air at the time of the announcement continued to their next destinations and were then grounded. The lock-out affected 68,000 to 80,000 passengers on the first day, with 600 flights canceled. It cost the airline more than $20 million each day. Given the impact this was having on the economy, the Australian Government applied to Fair Work Australia to act.

It issued orders that all industrial action taken by Qantas and the involved trade unions be terminated immediately, which brought the issue to an end. According to Qantas, the industrial action cost the airline A$194 million (US$195 million).

Tim Clark, more formally Sir Timothy Charles Clark – he was knighted for services to British prosperity and to the aviation industry – is another of those brilliant executives. He had started his career as a check-in clerk with British Caledonian in 1972 before moving to Gulf Air in Bahrain in 1975. Ten years later, the rulers of the Gulf state of Dubai asked him to become head of planning for a new airline. They said there wasn't much money, but they would give him $100 million to build the airline into something substantial.

Clark not only built an airline, he built an empire. Today, Emirates Airlines – Clark became president in 2003 – is one of the world's leading carriers, operating the largest fleet of giant Airbus A380 jets of any airline. It links destinations across the entire globe through its Dubai hub.

There are plenty of others, people like Jaime Bautista who headed Philippine Airlines (PAL). He was one of Asia's youngest airline CEOs at 47. PAL was another airline suffering financial trauma, and Bautista totally re-engineered its operations and brought it back to health.

And there were the men who led Singapore Airlines and maintained its reputation as one of the world's best airlines. Dr. Cheong Choong Kong, or Doc Cheong, served as Singapore Airlines (SIA) chief for two decades, retiring only in 2003. His successor was Chew Choon Seng, followed by Goh Choon Phong, who maintained the standard and led the carrier into a new age with the latest aircraft and increasing digitalization of the business.

Malaysian-born Tony Fernandes came from the music industry to launch LCC AirAsia, which was to become one of the world's most successful budget carriers. Fernandes had been with the Virgin Group before moving to Warner Music International London. At 28, he became the youngest person in recording industry history to head Warner Music Malaysia as its managing director, a role he excelled in. He later became vice-president of Warner's Southeast Asia operations before leaving the company in 2001 to start up AirAsia, which soon had offshoots across the region, in the Philippines, Japan, Thailand, India, Cambodia, as well as a medium- to long-haul operator, AirAsia X.

All those men, and many others, inspired me. They worked relentlessly, overcame major problems, and steered their companies through crisis. And all of them, and others, gave me their time. Some became friends.

People often say to me I'm an aviation expert. True, I've certainly picked up a lot of information over the years and can discuss the industry's issues at length. But I tell people that I'm not an expert. I'm just a reporter who interviews the experts and turns what they say into readable copy.

As I have said before, being a good reporter involves honesty, truth and, most of all, accuracy. If you are a journalist specializing in a particular field such as aviation, there is another critical element: trust. The people you are interviewing must trust you. If they do, they will speak more freely, even give you glimpses into their personal lives, their thoughts, and feelings. It helps add that touch of detail or color to a story. When you are speaking to an airline chief executive who trusts you, they will often tell you things 'off the record'. When they do, there can be two meanings. You must confirm which applies.

The first is that it is totally off the record, not to be written about under any circumstances. The second is that it is off the record in terms of not being directly attributed to the chief executive. However, you can use it in another way.

For example, if he tells you the airline is going to buy six new Airbus A350s but that's off the record because it hasn't been announced yet, you can still use it, but not say he said so. Thus, somewhere in the story you might write: 'The chief executive won't discuss fleet growth plans, but *Orient Aviation* understands the airline is considering purchasing at least six new-generation aircraft, probably Airbus A350s'. Building trust takes time but it is well worth it. But even chief executives come and go, and when one you have built a relationship with leaves, you start all over again with the new one.

My Herald days are behind me and globe-trotting with Orient Aviation magazine became the monthly assignment. Here, aboard an Airbus A350 on a test flight out of Toulouse over southern France.

17

Pandemic stress

Apart from the propensity of some airlines to self-destruct, global aviation has had to endure several crises not of its own making over the past few decades. I've been witness to most of them. There was Y2K, January 1, 2000, when the new century arrived and many thought planes would start falling out of the sky.

There were concerns about potential computer errors. Many programs represented four-digit years with only the final two digits, making the year 2000 indistinguishable from 1900. Computer systems' inability to distinguish dates correctly had the potential to bring down worldwide infrastructures for computer-reliant industries such as airlines.

In the event, it was a non-event, but it cost millions as airlines scrambled to forestall any problems. Then there was 9/11, the September 11, 2001, terror attacks in the US. People stopped flying in fear of further attacks. That was quickly followed by severe acute respiratory syndrome (SARS), which arrived in 2002, a global pandemic that caused passenger numbers to plunge. Some aircraft were flying near empty. From mid-2007 to early 2009, the global financial crisis plunged the world into economic stress. Again, travelers, and particularly business travelers, cut back on flying.

Then, in early 2020, the daddy of them all, COVID-19. The first cases of were identified in Wuhan, China, in December 2019, and the virus rapidly spread around the world. The World Health Organization (WHO) declared it a Public Health Emergency of International Concern on January 30, 2020, and a pandemic on March 11, 2020. The impact on aviation has been well reported.

Thousands of aircraft were grounded, parked at airports or at desert facilities in California or central Australia. Worldwide lockdowns and border closures made it almost impossible to travel. Airports were empty.

Airlines and airports stood down staff, and carriers canceled or postponed deliveries of new jets. The global airline industry lost an estimated $200 billion, and many carriers had to get financial assistance from their governments to survive.

Yet, despite the catastrophe wrought by the pandemic, airlines continued to do things they felt were vital to their future. They continued to invest in their industry-wide goal of sustainability, of reaching net-zero carbon emissions by 2050. They bought all the sustainable aviation fuel (SAF) available, even though it was three or four times the price of normal jet fuel. They even invested in planned new SAF projects and in green projects, such as tree planting. Given the losses they were suffering, it was clear evidence that despite widespread public criticism of aviation's impact on the environment and global warming, airlines were determined to play their part in efforts to solve the problem.

Not only airlines and the aviation industry suffered through the pandemic. It brought traveling to a screaming halt. My last overseas trip for what was to become three years was to Singapore in February 2020 to attend an airshow. I wouldn't normally have gone but for the Aerospace Media Awards – ASIA had called me and said I should take part in an awards dinner they were holding.

Even at that early stage, there were signs that COVID was becoming serious. People were wearing masks and using hand sanitizer. Temperatures were checked when you entered the air show. Before being allowed to enter a hotel, you had to fill out a form with all your personal details such as name, address, contact number, and a declaration you didn't have COVID.

At the awards dinner I soon discovered why they had been keen for me to attend. It was announced I was being presented with the Lifetime Achievement Award. It was a humbling moment, knowing years of work was being recognized by my peers.

The pandemic was to have a serious impact on our magazine. *Orient Aviation* was a relatively small business. We depended on advertising for revenue. Over the years, big companies like Boeing, Airbus, Embraer, Rolls-Royce, General Electric, Pratt & Whitney, engine lessors like Willis Lease Finance Corporation, even some airports and manufacturers of avionics or the sophisticated headphones worn by pilots, had advertised in the magazine.

It came to a screaming halt with the pandemic. Most companies simply stopped advertising. What was the point? And that left us struggling to survive, now a loss-making entity. We probably wouldn't have survived if it had not been for Publisher and Editor-in-Chief Christine McGee. She was a superwoman, working tirelessly to keep us afloat, putting her own money, not for the first time, into the business to keep it alive.

We went from a monthly magazine to publishing once every two months. We stopped printing the magazine and mailing it out to readers, saving on production costs, and moved to become an online publication. Because we were publishing fewer editions, we had a daily online digest, with brief stories of developments in the industry, which kept the brand alive.

And we took a personal hit. As a part-owner of the magazine, I had to do my share. I didn't get paid for months on end. Fortunately, I was in a decent financial position, which allowed me to bear the burden.

In terms of work, there was also a dramatic change. Like many cities around the world, Sydney was in lockdown for months. Residents couldn't leave the house except for medical appointments. Even when we were allowed to leave the house, we weren't allowed to leave our council district, which meant we couldn't even visit our daughter and son-in-law because they lived in a different council area. I certainly was not able to go to the airport and fly overseas, which would have been pointless anyway, given the restrictions that were in place virtually everywhere.

But there was a bright side. Modern-day communications meant I could do just about anything sitting in my home office that I would be doing out on the road. The face-to-face CEO interviews continued, arranged using Zoom, Microsoft Teams, or Webex. IATA and AAPA annual gatherings went virtual, meaning you could tune in over the internet and watch and hear everything that was going on. Indeed, IATA held weekly online press conferences hosted by Willie Walsh, former British Airways chief executive and now IATA director general, to brief us on the pandemic impacts, how airlines were handling it, and answer any questions the media had.

Yet another airline chief executive interview. This one with Emersiya Satar, chief executive of Garuda Indonesia Airlines. He was later jailed for accepting bribes.

It was a trying time for everyone but, somehow, we got through it. By the second half of 2022, many restrictions had been lifted, and most countries, though not all, had reopened their borders.

In Asia there were notable exceptions – such as China, where the pandemic had begun – and Hong Kong. COVID hadn't gone away, but most people had been vaccinated and were learning to live with it. The aviation industry, after the worst crisis in its history, was slowly recovering.

After three years, important industry events were no longer being held online. My first post-pandemic travel was in November 2022, to Bangkok to attend the AAPA Assembly of President, hosted by Thai Airways International. Meeting people you hadn't seen for several years, shaking hands, sometimes even hugging, was like some sort of return to normality. Though not quite.

A small group of us were invited to a briefing by Singapore Airlines chief executive Goh Choon Phong. When we entered the room, he was wearing a mask. 'Just to explain, I've had COVID,' he said. 'I'm clear now but better safe than sorry,' he added.

In early December, I had another trip, this time to Europe. There were two reasons. Airbus was holding an aviation summit to talk about developments, such as research it was doing into hydrogen-powered flight. The first day of the summit was in Toulouse and the second day in Munich. From there I had to go on to Geneva to attend

IATA's Global Media Days, the first in-person gathering since before the pandemic.

Airbus had booked me on a Cathay Pacific flight to London, transferring to a BA service to Toulouse. Airbus flew the media from there to Munich aboard one of its A350s, IATA bought me a ticket from Munich to Geneva. Airbus had arranged my return flight from Geneva to Zurich where I'd catch a Cathay flight to Hong Kong and Sydney.

It didn't quite work out that way. The weather in Geneva had been fine, very cold but fine … until the morning I was due to leave. When I looked out of my hotel room there was nothing but white. Snow blanketed everything. When I got to the airport and boarded the flight bound for Zurich there was a delay. The aircraft was covered with snow and had to join a queue of jets waiting to be de-iced. By the time we took off and landed in Zurich, my Cathay flight had already departed. Another night in Switzerland, I thought.

There was a long queue of stranded passengers at the transfer counter, all trying to arrange alternative flights. I had just joined the end of it when there was an announcement asking, 'Would Mr Thomas Ballantyne please come to the first-class counter.' That sounds promising, I thought. Unfortunately, it was not to be. Swissair had found me a way to get back to Sydney. It would be in economy all the way, with one of their flights to Dubai, then with Emirates back to Australia.

In the end, I arrived back in Sydney pretty much around the same time as I would have with Cathay, but it had been extremely tiring. The Hong Kong Government had regulated that if you are flying on Cathay, you had to wear a mask all the time, except while you were eating or drinking. Having to wear a mask for hours on end was suffocating. And, vaccinated or not, there was still a feeling of nervousness about being seated close to strangers. The fact that I felt so exhausted after that trip wasn't only because I hadn't flown for such a long period, nor because I was that little bit older. Something else had happened a year earlier that was to bring significant changes in my life.

18

Thoughts on the future

Do I worry about the future? Absolutely! Not for myself – for our daughter and generations to come. It is difficult not to be depressed when you watch the news each evening with coverage of the war in Ukraine and the Israel/Gaza conflict and the escalating threat posed by Russia, North Korea, and China.

Youngsters, even babies, dying senselessly, lives cut short by indiscriminate missiles hitting civilian targets. Famine in Africa. And global warming with severe weather causing chaos and disaster. Tornados in America. Typhoons in Asia. Tsunamis. Earthquakes and volcanic eruptions. Flooding and landslides. Unprecedented heat waves and bushfires. All of them, it seems, are happening more frequently. It's highly likely that wherever it all leads, I won't be around to see it, but you can't help but worry about all of it and where, ultimately, it will lead.

As for the airline industry, post-pandemic recovery is well underway. In many places air traffic is back to 2019 levels, and forecasts say passenger numbers will continue to rise, with Asia–Pacific leading the way. This, of course, assumes there is no future pandemic or other crippling crisis. And, given history, there is certainly no guarantee of that.

When airline chiefs met in Istanbul in June 2023 for IATA's annual AGM, the airline body's director general Willie Walsh told delegates the future looked pretty good. The message was slightly dampened by industry margins remaining wafer-thin. Walsh explained that, with $803 billion of revenues globally, airlines will share $9.8 billion in net profit in 2023:

> Put another way, airlines will make, on average, $2.25 per passenger. So, the value retained by airlines for the average plane trip won't even buy a subway ticket in New York City. Clearly that level of profitability is not sustainable. But considering we lost $76 per passenger in 2020, the velocity of the recovery is strong.

In Asia, while a few carriers are making record profits, overall, the region's airlines were also forecast to be in the red, with IATA predicting 2023 airline losses of $6.9 billion, although that would be half the $13.5 billion they lost in 2022. Nevertheless, for a global aviation industry that suffered its deepest losses in history – some $183.3 billion through 2020, 2021 and 2022 – the outlook is highly encouraging.

One of the biggest battles the industry will face is achieving sustainability, cutting its carbon emissions. At the 77th IATA AGM in Boston in October 2021, a resolution was passed by member airlines committing them to achieving net-zero carbon emissions from their operations by 2050. This pledge brought air transport in line with the objectives of the Paris Agreement to limit global warming to well below 2°C. Aviation wants to reach net-zero emissions by 2050. But aviation's target isn't set in stone. It is an aspirational goal and getting there will be far from easy.

IATA estimates that SAF could contribute around 65% of the reduction in emissions needed to reach the target. That will require a massive increase in production to meet demand. In 2023 the entire global production of SAF amounted to less than 2% of airline fuel requirements. Airlines are buying every last liter of it at four to five times the cost of normal jet fuel.

Aviation can't do it on its own. Government policy has an instrumental role to play in the deployment of SAF, and policies need to be harmonized across countries and industries. There must be incentives such as tax breaks, and investment by both governments and the private sector, to increase the production of SAF globally. To succeed, it will require the coordinated efforts of the entire industry (airlines, airports, air navigation service providers, manufacturers) and significant government support.

Other things that will contribute to this effort to become green are new technology, electric- and hydrogen-powered aircraft, infrastructure, and operational efficiencies, as well as offsets and carbon capture. Aircraft and engine manufacturers are all involved in research and development of such things as electric and hydrogen power, but the commercial aircraft that use these sources are decades away. Nevertheless, every new-generation jet that rolls off the production line is more fuel-efficient and less noisy than its predecessor.

Other, wider issues have dogged airlines for years. The International Civil Aviation Organization represents the world's civil aviation authorities, some 193 states. Getting them all to agree on something unanimously is nigh on impossible. International airlines want coordinated regulations. It is something they never get.

A prime example is security. After the 9/11 terror attacks in America, nations everywhere introduced new security measures. They were haphazard, different everywhere. Departing one country you had to take out your laptop computer and turn it on to show it was genuine. Somewhere else, you didn't. One place you had to take off your shoes and your belt. Not somewhere else.

Leaving Australia, you couldn't have anything in your toilet bag that held more than 100 grams. As I went through security, they pounced on a tube of toothpaste that said on the front it was 125 grams. It was half empty, probably holding less than 50 grams. It was confiscated. I've also had several small nail scissors taken away. Nonsensical. Security red tape gone mad.

There's something else. If I am flying from Sydney to Geneva, which I do at least once a year by way of Singapore and London, I go through security at Sydney. In Singapore, even though I am only in transit, I must go through security again. The same in London. That means three security checks on one trip, though you never leave the secure area of the airports or have any physical contact with the outside world.

Agreements should be reached between countries that allow them to accept the validity of the initial security check so passengers in transit don't have to go through it all again.

Air traffic regulations also cause airlines problems, and cost money. The rules vary from country to country. For example, the distance required between two aircraft flying in the same direction in an air corridor – the distance between the tail of the first aircraft and the nose of the following aircraft – is normally around 5 nautical miles, or 9.26 kilometers. But not always.

In some countries, it can be 5.5 nautical miles, or something else. It means as a flight crosses a border, it must speed up or slow down to meet the new rule. That means it is using more fuel as the engine is revved up or down.

Another beef involves passenger rights. Again, different countries have different regulations covering what an airline must do if a flight is delayed or canceled. If there is a delay or cancelation caused by something like a mechanical fault, most airlines want to keep their passengers happy. So, they arrange accommodation if the delay is overnight, and issue meal dockets.

What they do object to, quite rightly, is having to pay compensation or spend money if the delay or cancelation is caused by something they don't control, such as a severe weather event. Yet that is what some jurisdictions order them to do.

One thing is certain, traveling isn't going to get any easier over the coming years. It is hardly a hassle-free experience today, with security checks, congestion at airports, and flight delays. And as the number of people flying continues to rise, there will be immense pressure on the system. It is estimated that by 2028 the number of travelers flying around the world will reach around 5 billion; by 2040, 10 billion; and by 2050, some 15 billion. Coping with that is going to be a challenge.

But there is some hope. New technology is already arriving. Facial recognition is opening the way to a smooth passage through passport control, contactless check-in, and baggage drops. Body X-rays are being introduced to speed up security checks. And who knows what other new technology will come along to save the day and release the pressure.

19

Not quite the finale

All in all, I think I've had a charmed life. There have been high points and low points but that's part of the journey we all experience.

The three best days of my life had nothing to do with journalism. They were when I met Roz, when we married, and when our daughter was born. On the career front, I had come through three years covering guerilla conflict in Africa without a scratch. I had never had a broken bone. In more than seven decades, I had never spent a single night in hospital. That was about to change.

Roz and I had different doctors. When the COVID vaccination became available, my doctor wasn't administering it. Roz's doctor was. I changed doctors so that I could quickly get the vaccine.

I'm not sure how to describe Dr Ruth Mills. She was busy, wanting to ensure every aspect of your health was checked. You had to have a health plan, and she sent me off for all sorts of tests. One of them was a cardiac health check, though I had absolutely no symptoms or signs of any problems with my heart. It was November 2021. The test was conducted by her nurse, Elisha, and in less than a minute she looked at me and declared, 'You have an irregular heartbeat'.

After a hurried consultation with Dr Mills, I was sent straight over to see a nearby cardiac specialist, Professor Hosen Kiat, who conducted more tests, including ultrasounds, and an electrocardiogram (ECG), which measures electrical activity of the heart to detect cardiac problems.

I had severely blocked arteries, which probably shouldn't have come as a surprise since I had been a smoker for years. I could have suffered a heart attack or stroke at any moment, they told me. Within ten days, and with the pandemic still very much alive, I was in the Sydney Adventist Hospital in the northern Sydney suburb of Wahroonga, undergoing open-heart surgery, a triple-bypass operation. Luckily for me, it was performed by a brilliant heart surgeon, Professor Tristan Tang.

Of course, I can't remember any of it. I was literally out for the count. Professor Tang told Roz that she and our daughter could come and see me soon after the operation. I was still in the intensive care unit on life support and still out of it. They told me later I looked terrible, lying there with wires and tubes sticking out from various parts of my body.

For me, the worst part of it wasn't the operation, which I obviously don't remember; it was the week I had to spend in hospital recovering afterwards. The food was atrocious, tasteless. I couldn't eat most of it and lost several kilograms. After seven days of endless X-rays, tests, and lots of pills, they finally allowed me to go home. When my son-in-law Chris picked me up the first thing I said was, 'Take me to a Kentucky Fried Chicken. I need to get some food that has some taste.'

The washup of all this brought some major changes in our lives. I didn't go home but went to live with Tracey and Chris. This was because our house in Dundas Valley was on the side of a hill. There were steep steps leading down from the road to the front door, and more steep steps leading from the back door down to the backyard. With a six-month recovery period ahead, in my weakened state I couldn't handle the steps anymore. Their house in Baulkham Hills, west of Sydney, was on a flat block. Roz decided that we would have to sell our house and move to somewhere more suitable.

I don't think either of us imagined how traumatic the process would be. Finding a good real estate agent, and a conveyancing solicitor. Preparing the house for sale. We had been in the Dundas Valley home for around 40 years: four decades of collected belongings and detritus, some of which we had forgotten we even had. It was an old house, which required a lot of maintenance.

I was living in Baulkham Hills. Roz was still at our home. The Sydney property market was volatile. Prices were high but beginning to fall. An auction date was finally set but, in the event, didn't happen. We accepted a pre-auction offer which was higher than the guide price we had set. Then there was six weeks' wait before the sale could be settled, and the massive task of packing everything up, disposing of things we no longer needed, arranging a removalist.

The problem was, at that time, we had nowhere to move to. Our belongings had to go into storage until we found a new place. Where to go? Initially, we had thought of moving close to the kids, somewhere in western Sydney.

But then, we thought, no, let's look outside the city. In the end, it was the NSW Central Coast, an hour to an hour-and-a-half north of Sydney. We spent days and weekends traveling around, attending open houses, speaking to real estate agents in the area and inspecting homes. Finally, we found a property that seemed ideal: a three-bedroom lakefront home on Lake Budgewoi. We put in an offer, and it was accepted.

With daughter Tracey and son-in-law Chris.

However, nothing was going to happen quickly. The normal settlement period is around six weeks. We sold our house in late May and put in the offer on the new home in early June. But the owners didn't want to leave until August, when the man of the house was retiring. A three-month wait seemed excessive, but in the end, we decided it would be worth it. In the meantime, we continued to stay with Tracey and Chris. On August 17, 1992, we finally stepped through the door of our new property.

The wait was worth it. Although the intent had been to downsize, it didn't really work out that way. Our old house and the new house both had three bedrooms, but in the old house I had used one of the bedrooms as an office. This house had three bedrooms and a separate office. We now had an open-plan kitchen and living area downstairs and a large living area upstairs, compared to the single downstairs living room at Dundas Valley. Our new laundry was three times the size of our old one. We had a large double garage accessible directly from the house; in Dundas, a single garage, separate from the house. Best of all, downstairs there was a huge, covered deck at the rear of the house overlooking Lake Budgewoi ... and a wide covered balcony running the length of the house upstairs.

The backyard was completely enclosed, perfect for our dogs and our kids' dogs when they came to visit. And out the back gate each day, you could walk the dogs along the lakeshore: the perfect place to spend our twilight years, however long that may be.

Life is a fickle thing, full of what-ifs. If my mum and dad hadn't met during the war, I wouldn't be here. If my sister hadn't invited me on that guided tour of the *Scottish Daily Mail*, I may never have become a journalist. If my dad hadn't seen the ad for copy boys, I would probably have missed the opportunity. If there had been a job for me at *The West Australian* newspaper, I would never have met Roz, and if I hadn't been such a bad encyclopedia salesman, I wouldn't have got to know her better. If the French guy hadn't made suggestive comments about her, I wouldn't have written the letter that ultimately led to deep love and our marriage.

Later in life, if COVID hadn't erupted into a pandemic and I hadn't changed doctors to get the vaccine, my heart issue may never have been discovered, and it could have led to a stroke or heart attack. Of course, we will never know. Whether it's luck, kismet, fate or whatever, you eventually end up where you end up.

Do I have regrets? Of course. Introduce me to anybody in their mid-70s who doesn't have regrets. My greatest regret involves periods when I was at the SMH when I went off the rails. It was nothing to do with my career, which was going well.

It was to do with home life. The practice at the Herald after the day was done was for reporters to wander across the road to our local watering hole, the Australian Hotel. There we would chat about the day's events and discuss office gossip, of which there was always plenty. Clearly, we would drink copious amounts of beer. I would frequently get drunk. Very drunk. So drunk that I'd stagger back to the office and sleep there. Or climb into the back of my car and black out.

They were dreadful times for Roz and Tracey, who never knew where I was, what I was doing, or whether I'd be coming home. Not surprisingly, this put tremendous strain on our relationship. Roz could very easily have left me and taken our daughter with her. Somehow, miraculously, we got through it, but to this day, I am ashamed of how I acted at these times and how those actions threatened our marriage.

Looking back on the rest of it, I certainly can't complain. There were amazing highs, but also dreadful lows. I had a wonderful childhood with great parents. I found the love of my life, who is still with me, more than 50 years after we married. I had the career I wanted. Sure, I had been in prison but that was thankfully brief. I had sold encyclopedias, not very well, and tires. I have traveled to more than 50 countries, made friends, and experienced new cultures.

Journalism has let me report on conflict and tragedy but also joy, nearly every aspect of life on this planet. I met prime ministers, lords, knights, and celebrities, as well as ordinary people with ordinary lives who were having their 15 minutes of fame, whether it be good or bad. And the most extraordinary businessmen, the airline chief executives who somehow navigate their way through the most complex industry in the world.

I flew around our earth with the first man on the moon, and non-stop from Sydney to London years before it was commercially viable. It still isn't, though it is getting close. Oh, and I met Santa Claus. What more could a man ask of life?

About the author

Scottish-born (Edinburgh, 1947) Australian Tom Ballantyne, Associate Editor and Chief Correspondent of the Hong Kong-published *Orient Aviation* magazine, has more than 60 years of experience in international journalism. He began his career in the 1960s with the *Daily Mail* newspaper in that city, working for several other Scottish publications before moving overseas in 1969 to report on events in Australia and later Southern Africa.

During the early 1970s, Tom was a war correspondent for South Africa's *Argus* newspaper group, covering conflicts in Rhodesia (now Zimbabwe), as well as the Portuguese territories of Angola and Mozambique.

He returned to Australia in 1975 to begin an 18-year stint with that country's premier newspaper, the *Sydney Morning Herald*, covering a wide range of issues from industrial relations and crime to politics, defense, and feature-writing.

After three years as the Herald's CoS, he was appointed travel and aviation editor in 1989. During this period he authored *Breakfast in Bali, Supper at the Savoy*, a humorous travel tale, as well as co-authoring a second book, *A Year of Good Weekends* and co-authoring another humorous travel book, *Passengers who make your flight Hell! The lighter side of flying*.

After building a growing reputation as a specialist writer on the international aviation and airline industry, he left the Herald in 1995, working as Asia correspondent for the London-based *Airline Business* magazine before being appointed chief correspondent of *Orient Aviation*.

As well as writing, he has been a regular commentator on aviation issues on television and radio in Australia, Asia, the Middle East, and the United Kingdom, as well as on international aviation affairs for BBC World, Al Jazeera and CNN. Tom has also been a speaker at numerous aviation conferences and seminars.

Now based on the NSW Central Coast, an hour north of Sydney, Australia, he won the prestigious GE Aircraft Engines Award for the Best Air Transport Submission at the Royal Aerospace Society's Journalist of the Year Awards in London in 1998.

In 2000 he was a double winner in the Australian National Aviation Press Club annual awards, named the country's Aviation Writer of the Year, as well as author of the Best Aviation Feature Story of the Year. He has won the latter award five more times.

At a special function during the Singapore Air Show in February 2020, he was presented with the Lifetime Achievement Award by Aerospace Media Awards – Asia, and in 2023, given a Decade of Excellence award by the Australasian National Aviation Press Club.

Being presented with the Lifetime Achievement Award in Singapore, early 2020.

The award. Being recognized by your peers is always rewarding.

www.ingramcontent.com/pod-product-compliance
Lightning Source LLC
Chambersburg PA
CBHW060115170426
43198CB00010B/895